The Stillwater NewsPress
and the Stillwater Savings & Loan Association
are proud to present
D. Earl Newsom's carefully documented history
of the city that began one hundred years ago
in the Valley of the Still Water.

May the story it tells be treasured
and preserved by the generations that follow,
and may this limited edition record
of Stillwater's rich heritage inspire others
to carry on in the tradition
of its courageous pioneers.

James R. Bellatti and Lawrence F. Bellatti, Publishers,
and C. R. (Rick) Bellatti, Associate Publisher, the *NewsPress*
Bruce F. Webber, President,
Stillwater Savings & Loan Association

1889-1989 CENTENNIAL • THE OKLAHOMA LAND RUN
STILLWATER

Where Oklahoma Began!

A patriotic parade in May 1918 in the six
hundred block of South Main Street tells
several facets of Stillwater history. Leading
the parade are Wes Hesser, with the fife,
and his brother, Van, with the drum.
Behind them are two other brothers, Jake,
carrying the flag, and Jim. These are remnants of the Hesser family band that started
in the 1870s and carried on as a tradition
until World War I. In the background at
Sixth and Main is the Armory, where
troops drilled on the second floor.
Courtesy of the NewsPress
Pierce Collection

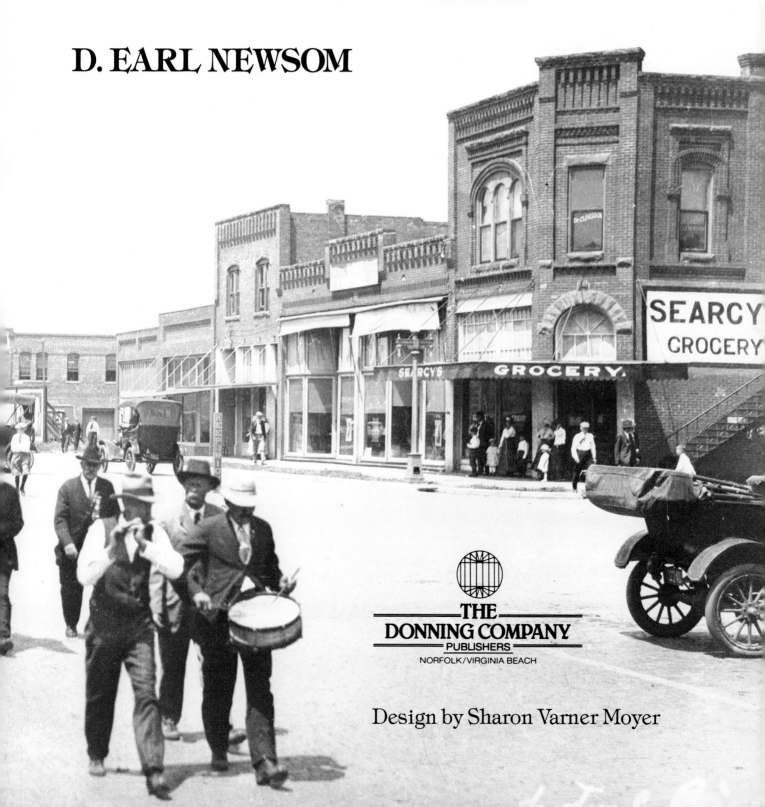

A Pictorial History

STILLWATER
ONE HUNDRED YEARS OF MEMORIES

D. EARL NEWSOM

THE
DONNING COMPANY
PUBLISHERS
NORFOLK/VIRGINIA BEACH

Design by Sharon Varner Moyer

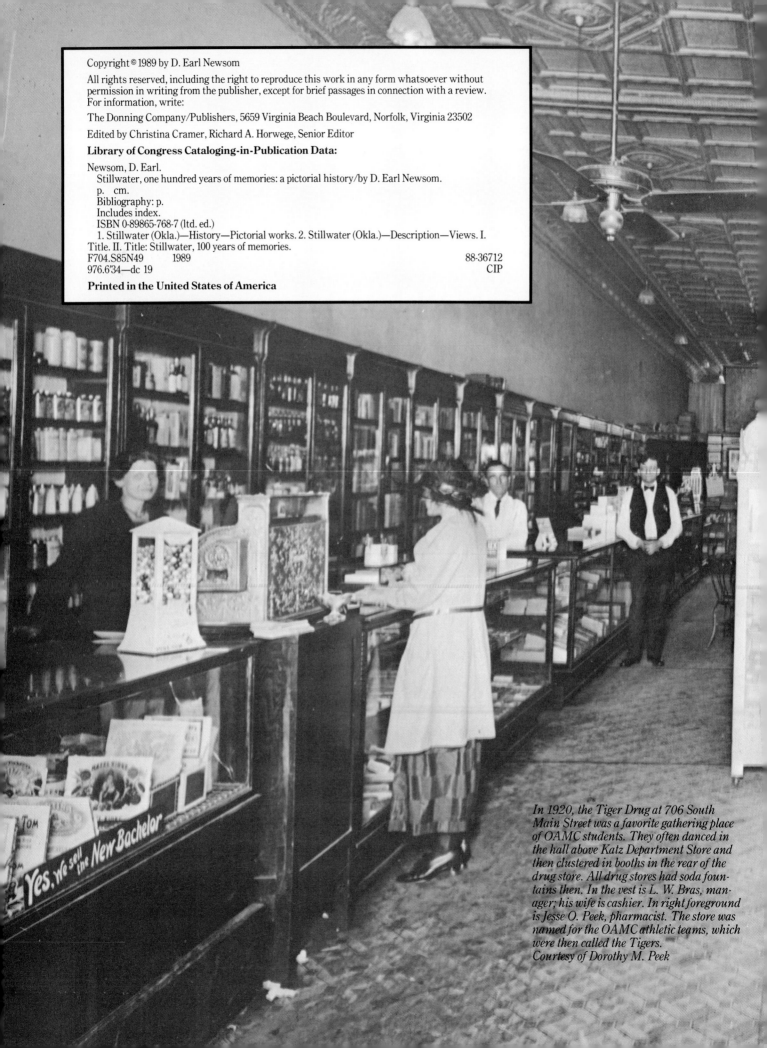

Copyright © 1989 by D. Earl Newsom

The Donning Company/Publishers, 5659 Virginia Beach Boulevard, Norfolk, Virginia 23502

Edited by Christina Cramer, Richard A. Horwege, Senior Editor

Library of Congress Cataloging-in-Publication Data:

Newsom, D. Earl.
   Stillwater, one hundred years of memories: a pictorial history/by D. Earl Newsom.
   p. cm.
   Bibliography: p.
   Includes index.
   ISBN 0-89865-768-7 (ltd. ed.)
   1. Stillwater (Okla.)—History—Pictorial works. 2. Stillwater (Okla.)—Description—Views. I. Title. II. Title: Stillwater, 100 years of memories.
F704.S85N49   1989   88-36712
976.6'34—dc 19   CIP

Printed in the United States of America

*In 1920, the Tiger Drug at 706 South Main Street was a favorite gathering place of OAMC students. They often danced in the hall above Katz Department Store and then clustered in booths in the rear of the drug store. All drug stores had soda fountains then. In the vest is L. W. Bras, manager; his wife is cashier. In right foreground is Jesse O. Peek, pharmacist. The store was named for the OAMC athletic teams, which were then called the Tigers.
Courtesy of Dorothy M. Peek*

DEDICATION

Dedicated to four men whose overwhelming endeavors and sacrifices meant so much to the founding and growth of Stillwater from a frontier village to a modern city:

David Lewis Payne, the Boomer leader and sometimes called the "Father of Oklahoma," who carved a trail to the Stillwater Valley and who dreamed of one day settling there.

William Lewis Couch, Payne's successor, who risked death and prison as he and his followers endured the bitter winter of 1884 on the banks of Stillwater Creek and called their encampment "the town of Stillwater."

Robert Arnold Lowry, who made the run of 1889, and then provided Stillwater with the brilliant leadership needed to secure the townsite, the county seat, Oklahoma A&M College, and other advantages that laid the foundation for the future of Stillwater.

Charles William ("Bill") Thomas, civic leader and mayor, who was active in almost every phase of Stillwater's development as it emerged as a modern city, but whose greatest contribution was bringing about the Kaw Water Project that may well permanently assure Stillwater of an adequate water supply.

Their achievements are told as part of this pictorial history.

The steam powered calliope sends its musical message that the circus has come to town on August 24, 1917. It probably performed on Charles Donart's farm in the Couch Park area or on the corner of Tenth and Adams, which was then in the country.
Courtesy of the Newspress
Pierce Collection

CONTENTS

For a time, a great custom of the country era carried over into the city years. The wise men of Stillwater gathered daily at Kate (Monty) Montgomery's Service Cafe to provide easy solutions to city, state, and national problems. At the first table are Clarence Cowan, Leroy Crossman, Mayor A. B. Alcott, Frank Berry, Walter Hoss, Warren B. Cooke, Dean Clarence McElroy, Roy T. Hoke, Sr., and Editor Marsden Bellatti; second table, Morris Gershon, Orville Mayfield, Floyd Turner, Kenneth Gallagher, Glen Varnum, Les McConkey, Burton Dix, Vernon Stark, Harley Thomas, and Herb Loyd (back to camera). Standing on the right, is "Monty." Courtesy of Clarence Cowan

FOREWORD

While virtually every community has an interesting and, to some extent, unique heritage, Stillwater's story truly is remarkable. For example, Stillwater played a major role both in the Land Run of 1889, which opened the Unassigned Lands in Central Oklahoma, and in the Run of 1893, which opened the Cherokee Outlet to non-Indian settlement. These land runs were amazing spectacles; indeed, they rank among the most dramatic events in American history. Yet, both are only a part of the mosaic of people, places, buildings, organizations, and events that have made Stillwater's history of one hundred years exciting and significant.

D. Earl Newsom's task was to capture Stillwater's heritage in words and images. Combining concise, readable and accurate narrative with over three hundred historic photographs, most of which have not been published previously, he has succeeded admirably.

Preparing pictorial histories may be likened to playing the guitar in that it is relatively easy to learn to play the instrument but exceedingly difficult to play it well. Likewise, it is fairly easy to produce a pictorial history with inadequate supporting text, and with photographs that are poorly chosen, illogically organized, and ineffectively captioned. Preparing an outstanding pictorial history, however, requires painstaking research, careful organization of text and photographs, effective narrative writing, and informative, descriptive captions. An experienced author, Newsom has taken all the necessary steps and thus has produced a fine book.

Stillwater: One Hundred Years of Memories actually is broader in scope than its title indicates, for the author effectively sets the stage for the creation of Stillwater by briefly reviewing the history of the region from 1541, when the Spanish Conquistador Francisco Vasquez de Coronado first entered the area that was to become Oklahoma, to the exploits of the Boomers. Moreover, after fifteen engaging chapters on the history of the city, Newsom offers the reader a glimpse of the "Plans and Dreams for 2010."

Both long-time residents and newcomers to Stillwater will find this book informative and entertaining. In addition, this book should have a wider audience, for it speaks to the universal dreams and aspirations of mankind. The founders of every community in Oklahoma—indeed in the United States—believed that their fledgling communities ultimately would become a prosperous city. Yet few of these settlements attained their goals and many became ghost towns. The story of Stillwater is one of initial struggle and ultimate success, and it should appeal to anyone interested in the history of Oklahoma, the American West, and the process of civic, social, and economic development. Everyone who played a part in making this project possible should be proud of the result.

Paul F. Lambert
Executive Director
Oklahoma Heritage Association

9

PREFACE

As Stillwater reaches the great milestone of its one hundredth birthday, this volume seeks to capture the highlights of its history and many of its precious memories over that long span. Too much has gone by to record every historical detail, and all the memories would fill countless volumes. But the pictures and stories herein should give residents, both old and new, a deeper appreciation and understanding of Stillwater's rich heritage. A brief sketch of early Oklahoma history is included as background for the Stillwater story.

Much of the material has been divided into chronological periods such as the early years, the "country years," and the years when Stillwater was growing into a city, but exceptions have been made at times in the interest of clarity or continuity. Several sources have been checked for most facts in the book. These include historical societies, museums, newspaper accounts, previous publications, and people who had reason to have special knowledge of happenings. I have learned from three previous historical books that, in spite of this, errors will occur. Even eyewitnesses and historians often disagree on what really happened, and documentary evidence may contradict what they both relate.

I am most grateful for the outpouring of help from so many individuals, which has made this book almost a community project. The cooperation was not surprising. Everywhere I did research, I found some group of Stillwater people working quietly helping others or doing something to make the community better for all. Beneath a quiet surface is a fierce pride in the home town and a desire to make it better.

Space does not permit mentioning all those who provided information or pictures. Under the photographs are names of citizens who joined the effort. If some individuals' names appear more than others, it is because they thoughtfully preserved historical material and pictures or because they gave much of their time to help make Stillwater history. The Donart family, for instance, was among the first

on the scene and each member became active in an important facet of Stillwater life. Robert A. Lowry was a leader in every project to ensure the village of a great future after the 1889 Land Run. In later years, C. W. ("Bill") Thomas and Roy T. Hoke were among those who gave generously of time and resources to help build a city.

Apart from pictures, some individuals have been especially helpful. When plans for this book were announced, Dr. Berlin B. Chapman wrote, "What you are doing is so important. You are authorized and welcome to use any or all of my pictures and research, and any other help that I can offer." I first met Dr. Chapman when I was administrative aide to U.S. Congressman Lyle H. Boren in the 1940s. He spent years in the National Archives doing research on Stillwater. He unearthed documents and correspondence that have provided the foundation for most of what has been written about early Stillwater to date. His 1948 book, *The Founding of Stillwater*, contains much of that material.

James R. Bellatti and Lawrence F. Bellatti, *NewsPress* publishers, and Rick Bellatti, associate publisher, have given the project enthusiastic support, and help has come from several staff members, including Scott Carter, Alice Church, Lawrence Gibbs, Gary Lawson, Paul Newlin, Larry Noller, and Dale Van Deventer.

I am convinced that Wilbur ("Bill") Simank knows more people who have lived in Stillwater than anyone else. Often when I sought information, the source would say, "I don't know, but I'll bet Bill Simank does." And usually he did. Bill's help was invaluable in getting the project underway.

Similar help came from Walter and Dianne Adams, Harry B. Bullen, John E. Duck, Brenda Esther Gould, John Greiner, Mr. and Mrs. Harold Jardot, Gertrude Vaughan Karr, Asa Lovell, Robert A. Lowry, Sam Myers, Emma Ingersol Price, Gene Ricker, Carol Rickstrew, Roland Selph, Dick Weilmuenster, and Fritz and Grace Donart Weilmuenster, all of pioneer families.

A special thanks is due Charlie Curtis. His father, Peter D. Curtis, homesteaded land adjacent to Payne Center, and he spent a great deal of time educating his children on the history of the area that they might pass it along to future generations. Charlie took me over the paths his father had walked with him.

Several Oklahoma State University specialists made important contributions. Kathleen Bledsoe of the Special Collections department, Oklahoma State University library, helped launch the project by locating many early day pictures and historical documents. Denise Rugg and Don Knight of the Audio Visual department copied those pictures and brought old photos to life. Dr. Ralph Hamilton's Public Information Office traced down several historic dates and events.

Only those who have visited Bill Thomas' home office can understand what a massive chore it was to go through his collection of historical material, but his wife, Virginia, was kind enough to do that. Similarly, Barbara Hartley Dunn, curator of Sheerar Museum and granddaughter of C. E. ("Elmer") Donart, searched through the museum and the Donart collection and found many historic pictures.

Carl Weinaug, city manager, offered the city's cooperation and pictorial scrapbook for this project and a number of his staff members were most helpful. These included John Wesley, David Hartman, Mike Shores, and Elton Nixon (all of the Community Development Department), Shelly Hartman, Linda Ely, and Mary Rupp. If you see fire hoses on streets in some pictures, it's because the fire department went through its files and found many photos. For these, thanks to Chief Jim Smith, Mary Tillman, and John Huff. William G. Nelson of the Parks and Recreation Department provided glimpses of the city's future.

A great deal of information about early Stillwater came from the Stillwater public library with the help of librarian John Augelli, who made all the library's resources available, and his staff, notably Richard Sutton and Marty Hoffman. One valuable source there was Clarence S. Bassler's vast collection of clippings and documents.

In 1934, Superintendent E. D. Price took it upon himself to do a history of the Stillwater school system. This and memoirs of Harry Donart, who taught in 1889, were helpful in compiling early school history. Dr. William E. Hodges, present superintendent, and Louise Richmond, clerk of the Board of Education, gathered information on the system during its later years.

Duane McVey, Payne County extension director, and Larry D. Poindexter of the Soil Conservation Service were sources for information on the status of agriculture, and Kelly P. Powell gave details on the story of his friend, Otto Gray. Our thanks to Robert E. Park, director of the Stillwater Medical Center, and Pat Webster, information specialist, for pictures of Stillwater Medical Center, and to Vonda Evans, for similar data on Indian Meridian Vocational Technical School.

Perhaps the most inspirational help came from Edna M. Couch, granddaughter of William L. Couch, the Boomer leader. A historian in her own right, she realized the importance of her grandfather to Stillwater's history. She not only encouraged this project but provided pictures of William L. Couch that have not appeared in previous books.

Otto Ramsey's grandfather owned the farm that became the Ramsey oil field. Otto drove me over the area and told me its history. Mrs. Cecil (Helen) Jones and Mrs. Mariann Miller, interim president of the Chamber of Commerce, followed with Ramsey field pictures.

Among others who provided information were Bill Bernhardt, Sr., Gerald Bradshaw, Rena Penn Brittain, Vivian Cagle, Margaret Cross, Hays Cross, Haskell Cudd, Mrs. Frank A. Dotter, Glenn Douglas, Ralph Dreesen, Mrs. Anna Frank Ferguson, Mrs. A. R. Flood, Mrs. and Mrs. Theodore Goldenberg, Hiram Henry, Mrs. Pauline Hooper, Winfrey D. Houston, E. E. ("Hook") Johnson, Dr. Robert B. Kamm, Sid H. Miller, Jonita Milligan, Charles E. Platt, Helen V. Posey, Father Don Smith, James M. Springer, Jr., Glenn Ward, Paul Wise, and Mrs. William R. Wright.

For the fifth time, Chandra Davis has typed a D. Earl Newsom manuscript; her excellent work and patience are appreciated. And for the fourth time, William Welge of the Archives and Manuscripts Division, Oklahoma Historical Society, dug deeply into the Society's collection for pictures. Joining in the picture search this time was John R. Lovett of the Western History Collections, University of Oklahoma.

And last, our thanks to Christina Cramer, editor for the Donning Company Publishers for her counsel along the way, and to Sharon V. Moyer, who created the design for *Stillwater - One Hundred Years of Memories*. Undoubtedly some kind and helpful people have been overlooked. This indicates no lack of appreciation—only that sometimes important details get lost among heaps of notes, files, and pictures.

D. Earl Newsom

Chapter 1

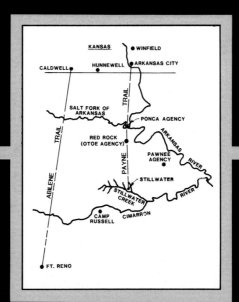

THE VALLEY OF THE STILL WATER

The stream that meanders along Stillwater's southern edge was once crystal clear. Wild game and trees bearing nuts and fruit flourished along its banks. The creek and its valley provided sustenance for travelers and Indians and a watering hole for cattle. The beauty of the valley amazed those who chanced upon it.

Washington Irving, author, storyteller, and traveler, provided the first recorded description of the creek and valley. Irving spent two days in the Stillwater area during his tour of the prairies in 1832. He camped first north of Ripley, where he described a "grand prairie" and "a singular crest of broken rocks resembling a ruined fortress" that reminded him of a Moorish castle. This rock structure stands today and is known as Washington Irving's Castle.

It was on Monday morning, October 21, 1832, that Irving and his party came upon the valley and the creek, which still had no name. He described it as "a deep stream running along the bottom of a thickly-wooded ravine." Although the banks were overgrown with trees, thickets, brambles, and grape vines, the travelers chose what appeared to be a suitable site for fording. Several of the horsemen slipped into water over their heads and Irving was snagged by a huge grape vine and thrown from his horse. The disaster was so ludicrous that it brought merriment to the group rather than anger. And as they emerged into the open, Irving wrote of the valley, "We now came out upon a vast and glorious prairie spreading out beneath the golden beams of an autumnal sun. The deep and frequent traces of buffalo, showed it to be one of their favorite grazing grounds...."

One legend says the Indians called the creek the Still Water because it was always still except during rain. Another states that cattlemen always found water "still there" year after year. But the creek finally received an official name in December 1884 when William L. Couch established his Boomer colony on its banks. The Boomers referred to the placid spring-like stream as the Still Water. They called their colony Stillwater.

The next description of the valley came on the Sunday morning of April 21, 1889, the day before the land run. Some homesteaders wept with joy as they looked down from a hill to the valley that would be their new home. John H. Barnes recorded the scene in his memoirs:

> We came upon a ridge north of where the airport is now. Just as the sun was going down, the clouds rolled back and the brilliant sunshine flooded...the Stillwater Valley. I do not recall ever seeing a more beautiful or more welcome sight. It seemed like the promised land, grass and trees were green, and wild flowers were springing everywhere. It was just a rolling prairie then with no sign of trees except around Stillwater Creek. Prairie grass, tall enough to hide a man on horseback, grew in the bottom land.... This grass had stems as big as one's little finger.

After the homesteaders rushed into the valley, the first newspaper, the Oklahoma *Standard*, appeared on August 3, 1889. In an article entitled "The Stillwater Valley," the publisher, Joe Merrifield wrote:

> Located in the northeast corner of Oklahoma...is the beautiful Valley of the Stillwater and in the fork made...with Boomer Creek is our lovely little city.... The fertile valley comprises almost 50,000 acres of as fine and fertile bottoms and upland as the sun shines on, traversed by treams and dotted with springs of clear, pure water, the smooth broad plains diversified with growths of the best and finest cottonwood, walnut, elms, and oak timber....

Among the charred ruins and decaying logs of the boomer's cabins, has…sprung into existence a beautiful city….The location is upon a gentle slope overlooking the Stillwater for miles, giving a magnificent view of valley, hill, forest, and good water that would intoxicate a landscape painter….Come to the Stillwater Valley…and its queen city, Stillwater….Begin life over again and grow up once more with a new and prosperous city…and have a hand in making it the best city in northeastern Oklahoma.

Much water has flowed through the Valley of the Still Water in the hundred years since those words were written. The prairie and rolling hills are covered with homes, buildings, and vegetation. Harsh words are sometimes spoken of the creek as it backs up and floods nearby city streets with muddy water. Its value may seem minimal, since for decades it has not been needed as a water supply. Citizens may find consolation in remembering that, except for the historic stream, there might not be a Stillwater, a county seat, or even a great university on what Washington Irving called "this glorious prairie."

Washington Irving provided a description of Stillwater Creek and other areas of Payne County more than a half century before the Land Run of 1889. Irving had spent seventeen years in Europe and was excited on his return in 1832 when invited to accompany a commission to treat with Indian tribes. He had long since completed his stories of "Rip Van Winkle," "The Legend of Sleepy Hollow," and other familiar works. Courtesy of the Archives and Manuscripts Division, Oklahoma Historical Society

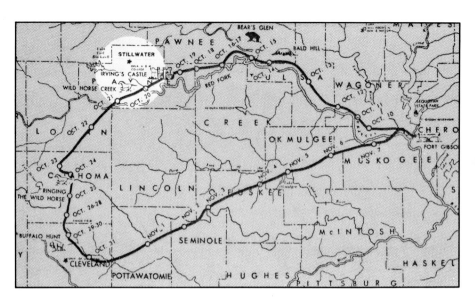

Washington Irving's journey through the Indian Territory started at Fort Gibson on October 10, 1832. Following the course of the Red Fork River, now known as the Cimarron, he reached the present Payne County area (in circle) on October 20. Few trees existed at this time except along the streams, and Irving had glowing praise for the "glorious prairie."
Map by Mike Shores, Community Development, City of Stillwater, based on an original map by George Shirk, 1955

From his campsite to the southwest, Washington Irving in 1832 described this crest of rocks as resembling a Moorish castle. He called it Cliff Castle. He also named the stream southwest of Stillwater Wild Horse Creek after a member of his party captured a wild horse there. David

Sherrill, the owner in 1889, never knew of Washington Irving and he hauled away some of the boulders, covered with Indian writings and drawings, to use for his farm pond dam.
Photo by the author

In December 1884, William Lewis Couch led a caravan of about two hundred Boomers down the Payne Trail from Kansas to the creek they called the Still Water. On Christmas Eve, the valley glazed with ice, Couch faced the rifles of thirty-nine U.S. cavalrymen. Told he would be shot if he refused to surrender or permit himself to be tied, Couch raised his Winchester and said the Boomers would fight. The U.S. Cavalry reconsidered and pulled-back. Couch's dream was that the Valley of the Still Water would become the first permanent settlement in the Territory. He was thirty-four then.
Courtesy of the Archives and Manuscripts Division, Oklahoma Historical Society

The first homestead certificate for Cliff Castle farm was issued to George Dollinger in 1895 and signed personally by President Grover Cleveland. Dollinger was appointed postmaster at Ingalls and never occupied the farm. In 1899 he sold it to David Sherrill for four hundred dollars. Sherrill's descendants still own the farm.

The Sherrills never knew the historical significance of the farm until 1931 when a family member recognized a description of it in Washington Irving's Tour On the Prairies. The farm has been closed to the public for many years, but in June 1988, the Daughters of the American Revolution held a ceremony at Cliff Castle and placed a plaque there designating it a historic site. Visitors are now welcome.
Courtesy of Marie Sherrill Rainwater

(4-401.)

THE UNITED STATES OF AMERICA,

To all to whom these presents shall come, Greeting:

Homestead Certificate No. 934

APPLICATION 3492

Whereas There has been deposited in the General Land Office of the United States a Certificate of the Register of the Land Office at *Guthrie Oklahoma Territory*, whereby it appears that pursuant to the Act of Congress approved 20th May, 1862, "*To secure Homesteads to actual Settlers on the Public Domain*," and the acts supplemental thereto, the claim of *George Dollinger* has been established and duly consummated, in conformity to law, for the *South East quarter of Section five in Township eighteen North of Range four East of Indian Meridian in Oklahoma Territory, containing one hundred and sixty acres* according to the Official Plat of the survey of the said Land, returned to the General Land Office by the Surveyor General:

Now know ye, That there is, therefore, granted by the **United States** unto the said *George Dollinger* the tract of Land above described: TO HAVE AND TO HOLD the said tract of Land, with the appurtenances thereof, unto the said *George Dollinger* and to *his* heirs and assigns forever.

In testimony whereof, I, *Grover Cleveland*, President of the **United States of America,** have caused these letters to be made Patent, and the Seal of the General Land Office to be hereunto affixed.

Given under my hand, at the City of Washington, the *twenty-fifth* day of *July*, in the year of our Lord one thousand eight hundred and *ninety-five*, and of the Independence of the United States the one hundred and *twentieth*.

BY THE PRESIDENT: *Grover Cleveland*
By *M. McKean*, Secretary.

L.Q.C. Lamar, Recorder of the General Land Office.

Recorded, Vol. *2*, Page *378*

Chapter 2

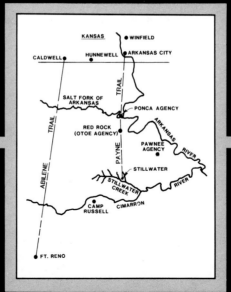

Within the map:

KANSAS

WINFIELD

CALDWELL ● HUNNEWELL ● ARKANSAS CITY

SALT FORK OF ARKANSAS

TRAIL

PONCA AGENCY

RED ROCK (OTOE AGENCY)

PAWNEE AGENCY

ARKANSAS RIVER

ABILENE TRAIL

PAYNE

STILLWATER

STILLWATER CREEK

CIMARRON RIVER

CAMP RUSSELL

FT. RENO

HOW OKLAHOMA BEGAN

To appreciate Stillwater's heritage, it is important that one understand how Oklahoma came about. The last great struggle to open the Oklahoma Territory to non-Indian settlement came on the banks of Stillwater Creek, and the first townsite in Oklahoma was located near there. The line from which the greatest land runs were made in 1889 and 1893 is now in Stillwater's city limits. These historic events were a climax to a story that began more than three hundred years earlier.

In 1541 San Francisco Vasquez de Coronado became the first white man to set foot on the land that was to become Oklahoma. A native of Salamanca, Spain, Coronado had been brought to Mexico in 1535 (then called New Spain) by the viceroy and his friend, Antonio Mendoza.

Tales were rampant in those days about fabulous treasures to the north, especially in seven large Indian cities called Cibola. After a special emissary sent by Mendoza found Cibola and looked down on the cities from a distance, he returned and convinced Mendoza that gold, silver, and precious stones could be found there.

Mendoza appointed Coronado leader of a large expedition made up of more than 250 horsemen and an army of adventuresome young Spaniards and Indians. The expedition left on February 23, 1540. Its goal was to locate Cibola and to bring back its riches.

After numerous delays, Coronado arrived at Cibola in July 1540 and, in a brief encounter, his forces overwhelmed the Zuni Indian inhabitants. The villages were located in what is now New Mexico. Coronado was crestfallen when he found no gold, silver, or precious stones. As he pondered what to do next, he sent expeditions to explore the surrounding country. One scouting leader, Hernando de Alvarado, returned from the Rio Grande Valley and Pecos pueblo with exciting news. A slave from a northern tribe being held by the Pecos Indians told of another fabulous city to the north called Quivira. Gold was everywhere in Quivira. Even utensils and dishes were made of gold. Small golden bells hung from trees and created sweet music. The story was a ruse by the Pecos Indians to get Coronado to leave, and it worked.

Coronado, however, remained in Cibola through the winter. Angered when the Indians rebelled against his occupation forces, he massacred several hundred of them. In May 1541, he embarked on his search for Quivira. The journey took him across what is now Oklahoma. His expedition passed through the western part of the state, then into Kansas.

With the Indian slave called the Turk as his guide, Coronado traveled east of Dodge City and found what he believed to be Quivira in northeast Kansas. Once again, he was bitterly disappointed. His find turned out to be only a Wichita Indian village of grass-covered huts with no trace of gold. Coronado's only consolation was to strangle the Turk, after which he headed empty-handed back to the comforts of home.

Meanwhile, another Spanish expedition headed by Hernando De Soto had reached into northeastern Oklahoma. De Soto's search for treasure started in Florida but eventually passed through Tennessee across the Mississippi River, through Arkansa, and into Oklahoma. De Soto is believed to have been within two hundred miles of Coronado's route.

The Spanish forays into Oklahoma by Coronado, De Soto, and later Juan Onate, are important because they represented the first non-Indian intrusions, they provided the first written description of life in the area, and they enabled Spain to lay claim to much of southern America. Oklahoma thus became a part of the Spanish Empire. The Spaniards had a profound effect on Indian life. The Plains Indians already camped in Oklahoma in 1541 were impressed with Spanish horses. The Indians became highly mobile as they quickly adopted this method of transportation.

For many years after this, Oklahoma was caught in a tug of war between Spain and France. The Spaniards established no colonies and the land continued to be a hunting ground for Indians until the French became interested in America in the 1600s.

The French established their first permanent colony in North America in 1608 at Quebec. Fifty years later, Louis Joliet and Father Jacques Marquette embarked on a twenty-five hundred-mile canoe trip that took them across Lake Michigan, and Green Bay, and then down the Wisconsin River to the Mississippi River, which they reached June 17, 1673. They continued to the mouth of the Arkansas River and then returned to Green Bay.

Joliet and Marquette set the stage for another expedition by Robert de La Salle. La Salle reached the mouth of the Mississippi and, on March 13, 1682, he took possession of the Mississippi Valley in the name of his king, Louis XIV. Oklahoma was a part of the land that La Salle named Louisiana. This was the same land already claimed by Spain.

The Spanish were upset by the claims and sent several expeditions to expel the Frence, but no contact was ever made and Oklahoma was destined to be under French rule for the next eighty years. Unlike the Spaniards, the French were traders rather than treasure hunters. They fanned out into many parts of their new land. The first of these to reach Oklahoma was Bernard de La Harpe in 1719. Operating with a base near the Red River, La Harpe led an expedition near to present day Haskell, Oklahoma. There he exchanged gifts with Indians as several thousand greeted his party. Other French traders followed La Harpe, including the Chouteau brothers, Auguste and Pierre, who had been trading with the Osage Indians in the Missouri Valley.

In 1763, the Oklahoma lands were returned to Spain. France suffered great losses during the French and Indian War of 1756. The heavy expense of maintaining her North American possessions, and the probability that she might lose Louisiana anyway, caused Louis XV to make a gift of the entire area to Spain, his ally in the war. Spain refused the gift for a time. The Spanish said they already owned the land, but in 1766 they accepted.

Spanish possession of Louisiana, which still included Oklahoma, was not to last. After the American Revolution against England and the subsequent adoption of the Constitution in 1788, the newly freed United States colonies began to expand westward. A quarrel ensued with Spain over rights of the United States to use New Orleans as a port. Almost simultaneously, the Spanish became involved with England over rights to Pacific Coast lands. Adding to her problems was the rise of Napoleon Bonaparte to power in France. Napoleon wanted Louisiana back in French domain and in 1800 he pressured Spain into ceding the American province back to France.

Oklahoma was once more included in the treaty and was again under French rule. This, too, was to last only a short while. When Thomas Jefferson was elected president in 1801, he was deeply concerned about having a province in North America controlled by Napoleon, and he wanted New Orleans accessible as a United States port. Jefferson decided to buy New Orleans from the French, but Napoleon needed money to support his army and his conquests and he offered to sell all of Louisiana. Jefferson accepted and in 1803 closed the deal for $15 million. The Louisiana Purchase was criticized by Jefferson's enemies, but it laid the foundation for the United States becoming a great nation and a world power.

The Purchase also ended the first phase of Oklahoma history. No longer would the land be passed back and forth between Spain and France. Thanks to Jefferson, the Oklahoma land was now a part of the United States of America. It was still virtually a virgin land. Neither the French nor Spanish had established permanent colonies. It was much as Coronado had found it—a land populated by herds of buffalo and a few Indian tribes, with an abundance of game, fish, and beautiful streams.

Francisco Vasquez de Coronado found no treasure at the end of his journey across Oklahoma in 1541, but he erected this cross at Quivira, Kansas. After strangling the guide who had deceived him, Coronado spent twenty-five days in Quivira before returning to Mexico City.
From A History of Kansas, *1920*

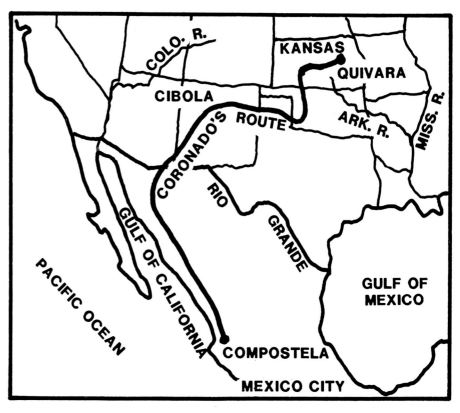

Coronado took this route from Mexico City to the Seven Cities of Cibola in New Mexico and then through western Oklahoma. He was the first non-Indian to travel Oklahoma. His impressions of the land conveyed to Emperor Charles V of Spain were largely negative. He ran out of corn and water, had to cook food over cow dung, and often became lost on the vast prairie.
Drawing by Dwight Zimbelman

A graduate of West Point, Col. Auguste Pierre Chouteau established the first legal trading post in Oklahoma in 1817 at Salina. His father, Pierre, had made earlier history in 1802 by establishing the first white man's residence in Oklahoma and an unauthorized trading post on the Arkansas River at its junction with the Grand and Verdigris rivers.
Courtesy of the Archives and Manuscripts Division, Oklahoma Historical Society

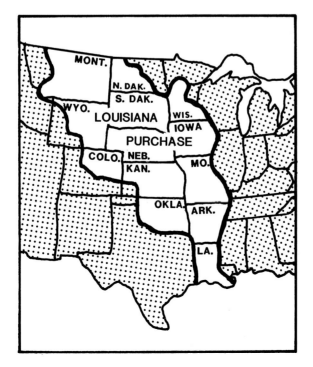

As historians traced Washington Irving's tour route in 1955, they also stopped at the site of Pierre Chouteau's trading post. When Irving arrived there in 1832, he was greeted by his friend, Col. Auguste P. Chouteau, Pierre's son. In front of the historical marker are, left to right, Gen. W. S. Key, then president of the Oklahoma Historical Society, Dr. B. B. Chapman, center, and Paul Masse of New York. The two at far right are unidentified. Historians usually cite 1892 as the date of the trading post founding.
Courtesy of Dr. B. B. Chapman

Oklahoma was caught in a tug of war between France and Spain for many years, but when Pres. Thomas Jefferson concluded the Louisiana Purchase in 1803, it became a part of the United States. The vast area of the Purchase is shown above.
Drawing by Dwight Zimbelman

Chapter 3

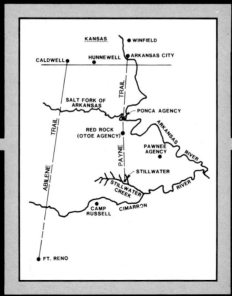

KANSAS

WINFIELD

CALDWELL HUNNEWELL ARKANSAS CITY

TRAIL

SALT FORK OF
ARKANSAS

PONCA AGENCY

RED ROCK
(OTOE AGENCY)

ARKANSAS

PAWNEE
AGENCY

RIVER

PAYNE

STILLWATER

STILLWATER
CREEK

RIVER

ABILENE

TRAIL

CAMP
RUSSELL

CIMARRON

FT. RENO

THE FIVE CIVILIZED TRIBES ARRIVE

The removal of the Indian tribes from their eastern homes to the Indian Territory is one of the tragic chapters, not only in the Oklahoma story, but in the history of the nation as well. The removal resulted not only in great strife between tribes and the U.S. Government, but caused great dissension and even murders within some of the tribes. The journeys of the Indian tribes to their new homes are still known as the Trails of Tears.

Scarcely had the American colonies pulled themselves together under a new constitution in 1788 than whites began moving onto lands occupied by the Five Civilized Tribes in southeastern United States. These tribes (the Choctaws, Cherokees, Creeks, Chickasaws, and Seminoles) were called thus because they had achieved a reasonably high level of living and culture even before white expolorers touched American soil. Their governments, farms, and homes were impressive.

The Creeks occupied nearly ten million acres in Alabama and Georgia; the Cherokees held more than seven million acres in Georgia, Alabama, and Tennessee. The Choctaws, Chickasaws, and Seminoles occupied lands in Mississippi and Florida.

Each tribe considered itself an independent nation and not subject to control by the states in which they were located. The neighboring whites coveted the Indian lands. They looked with anxiety and suspicion on the Indians and refused to accept the Indian concept of independence.

In 1828, Georgia enacted legislation which annulled Cherokee laws and asserted the state's sovereignty over the Indians. Other legislation in 1829 and 1830 gave the State of Georgia possession of Cherokee lands and stripped the Indians of personal and property rights. When the courts upheld these actions, pressures grew to move the Indians out of the area.

President James Monroe had in 1824 asked Congress to establish a territory for the Indians, and subsequently President John Quincy Adams supported the move. President Andrew Jackson was even more determined to remove the Indians and he approved Georgia's actions. In 1830, he signed what was called the Removal Act into law. It established a vast area of land in the West called the Indian Territory. The Five Civilized Tribes would be given homes there in exchange for their lands in the southeastern United States.

Some of the tribes had already made treaties by the time the new law became effective. The Choctaws in 1820 had agreed to give up lands in Mississippi and Alabama for a large area in southern Oklahoma, although many of them refused to leave. Other tribes signed treaties during the next fifteen years.

Many Creek Indians were bitterly opposed to leaving their lands in Georgia and Alabama and moving to the Indian Territory. When the Lower Creeks faction signed a treaty in 1825 trading their land for a large tract between the Arkansas and Canadian Rivers, the Upper Creeks and their chief, Opothleyahola, refused to honor the treaty. They sentenced the chief signer, William McIntosh, to death and shot him as he tried to escape from his burning house. The Creeks signed another treaty in 1832 agreeing to move west.

The Seminoles of Florida were even more bitter about a treaty made in 1832 for their transfer to the new territory. Chief Osceola rallied the tribe and fought the United States. During the war, he hid women, children, and elderly tribesmen in Florida's swamps. Federal troops followed a "scorched earth" policy and destroyed the homes, possessions, and cattle of the Seminoles. Under the guise of truce talks, they took Osceola prisoner and he died at Fort Moultrie. The majority of the Seminoles, some 4,000, later settled in the central part of the Indian Territory.

In 1832 the Chickasaws, faced with the growing intrusion of white settlers, ceded their Mississippi lands to the United States in exchange for a home in the new Indian Territory. This left the Eastern Cherokees in Georgia as the last major hurdle for negotiators. The hurdle was a great one. The Cherokees were a highly civilized tribe with their own homes, farms, businesses, and newspapers.

When the Georgia legislature assumed domain over the Cherokee Nation, the tribe appealed to President Jackson, but he turned a deaf ear. The pressures were strong for the Cherokee to abandon their homes and to move west, but most did not want to go. The Western Cherokees had already traded Arkansas lands for what became known in Oklahoma as the Cherokee Outlet, but the Eastern faction resisted and pleaded to keep their Georgia holdings.

Their hopes were dashed when a small Cherokee delegation on December 29, 1835, signed a treaty at New Echota, Georgia, giving up Cherokee lands east of the Mississippi River for five million dollars and lands in the West. Three of those who signed the treaty, Major Ridge, his son, John, and Elias Boudinot, were later assassinated. The incidents divided the Cherokees into two factions for years.

With the signing of the Removal Act and the treaties, the United States government began removing the reluctant Indians to their new western home. Their tragic journeys to the Indian Territory have been called the Trails of Tears. Between 1831 and 1834, thousands of Choctaws died along the route through Mississippi from sickness, exposure, and homesickness.

As many as four thousand Cherokees, including chiefs, met a similar fate as they traveled in groups of one thousand through parts of Kentucky, Tennessee, and Missouri after having given up their homes in Georgia. By the spring of 1839 most of the survivors arrived at their destination and started life again in the new Indian Territory.

The Indians lived in relative peace for the next two decades, although they sometimes faced attacks from the Plains Indian tribes, notably the Comanches. They built log homes, raised crops and livestock, and many adopted white men's clothing. They established schools and some Indians sent their young to academies outside the territory. The Cherokees developed a public school system. Christian missionaries moved into the area. The development of the tribes was remarkable. The Indians became more friendly toward the federal government as the wounds of the Trails of Tears began to heal.

All this changed in 1861 when the Civil War began. Old wounds among the Cherokee and Creek factions were reopened, and Indians found themselves fighting each other in battles between the Union and the Confederacy. The majority of the tribes, however, aligned themselves with Confederate forces. Most of the tribes owned slaves and wanted to keep them. Intermarriage with southern whites had occurred frequently. The Indians felt a kinship with the South in spite of earlier hardships.

Of special importance to Stillwater's history was the Battle of Round Mountain. This was the first major battle of the Civil War fought in Oklahoma and one of the most tragic. The Payne County Historical Society has erected an historical marker sixteen miles east of Stillwater to commemorate the site.

The battle occurred on November 19, 1861, as Opothleyahola, chief of the Upper Creek faction, decided to cast his lot with the Union. Ill-equipped for fighting and with many women and children in his camp, he sought to make his way to Kansas. He was overtaken at Round Mountain by Col. Douglas H. Cooper's Confederate troops, which consisted largely of Creek, Seminole, Choctaw, and Chickasaw Indians.

Opothleyahola lost more than one hundred men and much property in the battle but escaped at night and continued his flight toward Kansas. He was pursued and attacked at Bird Creek and again on December 26 just south of the Kansas line. His forces were devastated and broken up into small groups.

When remnants of the expedition finally crossed into Kansas, they were bleeding, frozen, and barefoot, and several hundred had been killed. More than one thousand Indian ponies died during the conflict. Opothleyahola himself died a few months later, but the suffering his people endured aroused Kansas and inspired the organization of a large Union expeditionary force. The first battle is said to have affected the course of the entire war in the Indian Territory.

The Seminoles of Florida signed a treaty in 1833 agreeing to move west. A few accepted the treaty but other Seminoles were bitterly opposed to the removal. A young subordinate chief, Osceola, carried on a war against the United States and won national attention when his warriors won several encounters. Unable to conquer the Indians who hid in the Florida swamps, the government authorities lured Osceola to a truce conference and then imprisoned him. His spirit broken after the deception, he died in prison in January 1838. The Seminoles were overcome and were moved to the Indian Territory in 1842.
Courtesy of the Western History Collections, University of Oklahoma

Perhaps the most revered statesman and principal chief in Choctaw Indian history, Pushmataha was a leader in negotiating treaties with the United States by which the tribe ceded its lands in Mississippi for a new home in the West. In the War of 1812, Chief Pushmataha had fought with Gen. Andrew Jackson, the government's principal negotiator for Choctaw lands in 1820. He had also fought under the United States flag in actions against the Creeks and Seminoles.

Chief Pushmataha was a shrewd negotiator and won for the Choctaws nearly all of southern Oklahoma in exchange for their Mississippi lands. He died in 1824 during treaty negotiations and was buried in the Congressional Cemetery with high military honors. Pushmataha County in Southeastern Oklahoma was named for him.
Courtesy of the Archives and Manuscripts Division, Oklahoma Historical Society

Elias Boudinot, whose Indian name was Buck Watie, was assassinated on June 22, 1839, in the Indian Territory. Angered because Boudinot signed the Treaty of New Echota in 1835 forcing the Cherokees to give up their eastern lands, a group of his own immigrant tribesmen tied his hands and cut him to death with knives and tomahawks.

Educated in Connecticut, Boudinot was founder and editor of the Cherokee Phoenix *in New Echota, Georgia, which the Cherokees in 1825 had designated their permanent capital. His newspaper was widely distributed to congressmen and influential citizens to gain understanding and support for Cherokee causes. His son, Elias C. Boudinot, eventually became a powerful leader in the tribe.*
Courtesy of the Archives and Manuscripts Division, Oklahoma Historical Society

Major Ridge was leader of what was known as the "Ridge faction" of the Cherokees that signed the Treaty of Echota ceding tribal lands in Georgia to the United States in exchange for lands in the Indian Territory. His faction represented a minority of the tribe and he was accused of collaborating with Gen. Andrew Jackson and Georgians who coveted Cherokee lands.

On June 22, 1839, after he had emigrated to the Indian Territory, Ridge was shot and killed about 10 A.M. by a sniper as he traveled along an Arkansas road. The murders of Ridge, his son, John, and Elias Boudinot, created a furor throughout the Indian Territory and caused bitterness for years among factions of the Cherokee tribe.
Courtesy of the Archives and Manuscripts Division, Oklahoma Historical Society

John Ridge, son of Major Ridge, was also a victim of the June 22, 1839 assassinations. In 1830 he fought the government's efforts to force the Cherokees to give up their Georgia lands, but in 1835, he came to believe the removal was inevitable and signed the Treaty of Echota. He was stabbed to death at his home in the Indian Territory while his wife and children watched. He and his cousin, Elias Boudinot, had been educated together in Connecticut.
Courtesy of the Archives and Manuscripts Division, Oklahoma Historical Society

Peter Perkins Pitchlynn and Nitakechi, nephew of Chief Pushmataha, led the Choctaws from Mississippi to their new home in the Indian Territory. The Choctaws were the first to begin their "Trail of Tears" in 1831. Their removal was completed in 1834. Pitchlynn became principal chief of the tribe. When the Civil War began in 1861, he sympathized with the Union but his people overwhelmingly wanted to join the Confederacy. When the war ended, he surrendered the Choctaw forces to the government on June 19, 1865. He represented the tribe at the great Fort Smith Council in September 1865.
Courtesy of the Archives and Manuscripts Division, Oklahoma Historical Society

The Creek Indians, like most of the other Five Civilized Tribes, were bitterly divided over ceding their Georgia lands to the United States and moving to the Indian Territory. In 1825, William McIntosh of the Lower Creek faction, made a treaty giving up the Creek lands. On April 30, a hundred warriors led by Opothleyahola of the Upper Creeks set fire to the McIntosh home. When McIntosh emerged, he was shot and killed. The Creeks eventually moved to the Indian Territory and several thousand perished en route.
Courtesy of the Archives and Manuscripts Division, Oklahoma Historical Society

Daniel N. (Dode) McIntosh, whose father, William, was murdered in Georgia after signing the Creek removal treaty, became a leader of the Creeks in the Indian Territory. He commanded a Creek regiment for the Confederacy during the Civil War. He headed the Creek delegation to the Fort Smith Council just after the war and went to Washington to help negotiate the Treaties of 1866.
Courtesy of the Archives and Manuscripts Division, Oklahoma Historical Society

Stand Watie's name is among the most prominent in Cherokee Nation history. Born near Rose, Georgia, December 12, 1806, he was a brother of Elias Boudinot. He was among those who signed the Treaty of Echota in 1835 but escaped his would-be assassins on June 22, 1839, in the Indian Territory.

After the assassinations of Major Ridge and his son, John, Watie became the most influential leader of the Ridge faction of the Cherokees. When the Civil War began in 1861, he organized and was made captain of a special force guarding Cherokee lands against raids of Union forces in Kansas. In May he was made a captain in the Confederate army and on May 16, 1864, he was promoted to Brigadier-General by Pres. Jefferson Davis of the Confederacy. Watie served with distinction and when the Confederate cause was lost, he was honored by being assigned to surrender the last Confederate troops at Doaksville in the Choctaw Nation on June 23, 1865. He died September 9, 1871.
Courtesy of the Archives and Manuscripts Division, Oklahoma Historical Society

Although he was only one-eighth Cherokee and never mastered the tribe's language, John Ross was principal chief and revered Cherokee leader for forty years. He helped write the Cherokee Constitution in 1822. He represented the majority of the tribe opposing the removal to the Indian Territory from Georgia. He led the Cherokees in prayer as they began the Trail of Tears in 1838 and made the trip to the Territory. Despite measures Chief Ross devised to protect the Cherokees, thousands suffered death and disease on the journey.

Ross was blamed by Elias C. Boudinot and Stand Watie for the assassinations after the New Echota Treaty and once sought protection from the government when he thought Watie would attempt to murder him. Oklahoma historian Grant Foreman termed Ross "one of the great men of America of his day." Ross is shown here with his wife, Mary. He died in 1866.
Courtesy of the Archives and Manuscripts Division, Oklahoma Historical Society

Each of the Five Civilized Tribes experienced its "Trail of Tears," starting with the Choctaws in 1831, but the term is popularly associated with the sixteen hundred mile journey of the Cherokees from Georgia to the Indian Territory during the winter of 1838. Of the sixteen to seventeen thousand who made the journey, four thousand were reported to have perished. Elizabeth Janes captured some of the suffering of the Indians in her painting, "Removal of the Civilized Tribes to Oklahoma." Congress has designated the route as a National Historic Trail.

Courtesy of the Archives and Manuscripts Division, Oklahoma Historical Society

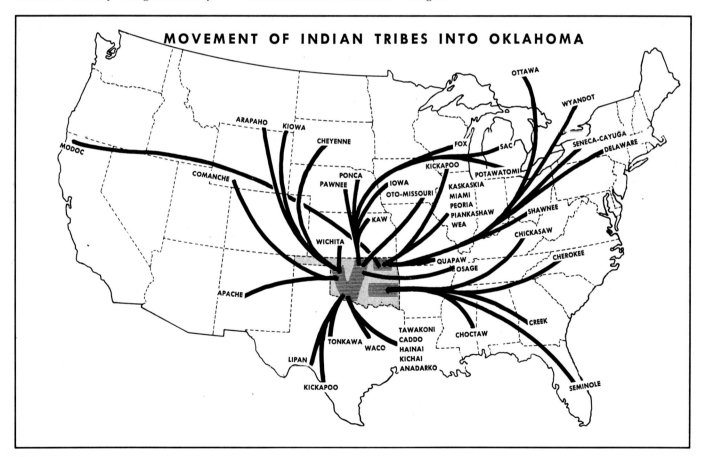

MOVEMENT OF INDIAN TRIBES INTO OKLAHOMA

The Indian Removal Act of 1830 and a series of treaties starting in 1827 were the beginning of a movement that made Oklahoma a territory for Indians. This map shows the original homelands of some tribes. The original Indian Territory was much larger but became limited to Oklahoma after Nebraska and Kansas achieved statehood. The migration of the Choctaws and Cherokees to the new land became known as the Trails of Tears.

Map Courtesy of the Division of Indian Health, U.S. Public Health Service

Often considered the most famous of all Cherokees is Sequoyah, whose statue is now in the Hall of Fame in the national capitol building in Washington. Impressed by white men's ability to write, Sequoyah worked from about 1809 to 1821 devising an alphabet or syllabary of eight-five characters that represented sounds in the Cherokee language. His alphabet brought about the printing of books and newspapers and broader education for the Cherokees.

After Sequoyah came to the Indian Territory, some Cherokee parents sent their children to him to learn reading and writing. In 1902, an effort began to obtain statehood for the Territory and to have it named Sequoyah but Congress rejected the proposal. Sequoyah's father was Nathaniel Gist, a white man, and Sequoyah went by the name George Guess.
Courtesy of the Archives and Manuscripts Division, Oklahoma Historical Society

As the Civil War began in 1861, the Choctaws quickly sided with the Confederacy, since many of them were slave owners. On June 10, 1861, the tribe's General Council declared the Choctaw Nation free and independent and appointed a commission to make an alliance with the Confederate States.

Among the first to join the Confederate forces was Tandy Walker, former Choctaw Nation governor. He was probably recruited by Col. Douglas H. Cooper, who had been a Choctaw agent for eight years. Walker became a colonel and commander of three regiments that constituted the Second Indian Brigade. The brigade was praised for gallant action in the spring of 1864 after it volunteered for action under General Sterling Price in an Arkansas campaign.
Courtesy of the Archives and Manuscripts Division, Oklahoma Historical Society

A veteran of the Mexican War and a friend of Pres. Jefferson Davis of the Confederacy, Col. Douglas H. Cooper commanded the Confederate troops at the Battle of Round Mountain in November 1861. His force of fourteen hundred men consisted largely of Indians who had joined the Confederate cause. Courtesy of the Archives and Manuscripts Division, Oklahoma Historical Society

In charge of the Creek forces loyal to the Union at Round Mountain was Opothleyahola, former chief of the Upper Creek faction. Burdened with many women and children in his expedition, he knew his only hope was to escape into Kansas. Colonel Cooper's army overtook him at Round Mountain and inflicted heavy casualties. Courtesy of the Bureau of American Ethnology, Smithsonian Institution

The Round Mountain battle site has been disputed, but the Payne County Historical Society believes its documentary evidence shows beyond a doubt it was about sixteen miles east of Stillwater near the twin mounds visible in the background of this photo. Here, on December 30, 1955, John H. Melton, director of research for the society, center, and Dr. B B. Chapman, its president, on the right, began building a historical monument to commemorate the site, which is now often referred to as "Twin Mounds" and "Round Mountain(s)." At left is Sherman T. Kerby, donor of the site on old Highway 51.
Courtesy of Dr. B. B. Chapman

Several thousand attended a special ceremony on April 15, 1956, dedicating a monument erected by the Payne County Historical Society to mark the site of Round Mountain(s), the first Civil War battle in Oklahoma. On the platform, left to right, are Dr. B. B. Chapman, Frank B. (Pistol Pete) Eaton, and Don Holton, who held a caricature of Pistol Pete which became the official Oklahoma State University emblem.

Behind the platform was an Oklahoma A&M College honor guard. Near the truck in civilian clothes was John H. Melton, who instigated the research that led to identifying the battle site.
Courtesy of Dr. B. B. Chapman

This sketch by James R. O'Neill, that appeared in Leslie's Weekly, August 1863, depicts the Battle of Honey Springs. On July 17, 1863, at Elk Creek (or Honey Springs) about twenty miles south of Fort Gibson, Union troops commanded by Gen. James Blunt won a decisive victory over Confederate forces of Douglas H. Cooper, who had been made a brigadier general in May. The battle involved several thousand men in both armies. The Confederate defeat left many Choctaws and Cherokees suffering from hunger and disease, and many perished.
Courtesy of the Archives and Manuscripts Division, Oklahoma Historical Society

The Cherokee National Capitol Building at Tahlequah appears today much as it did when built after the Civil War. The Cherokee Council first met in a shed on the site in 1839 and organized the town in 1843. The log cabins they built were burned during the war by the Confederate Cherokee leader, Stand Watie. The building is now a popular tourist attraction.
Courtesy of the Archives and Manuscripts Division, Oklahoma Historical Society

Chapter 4

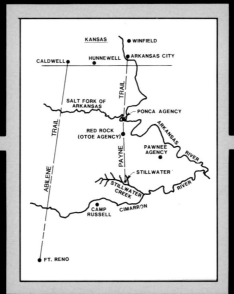

THE BOOMERS CARVE A TRAIL TO STILLWATER

As soon as the Civil War ended, the government called the Indians to a great council in Fort Smith, Arkansas. By siding with the Confederacy, the tribes had forfeited their treaty rights and even their property could be confiscated. The government wanted to work up a plan to renew relationships with the Indians. Thousands of Indians, including many distinguished chiefs, gathered for the council on September 8, 1865.

Dennis W. Cooley, superintendent of Indian Affairs, told the Indians the government wanted them, especially the loyal tribes, to have homes, but they must free all their slaves. The Indians were somber. For more than thirty years they had lived in the Territory the government had traded them for their lands in Georgia, Florida, Mississippi, and Arkansas. Now they sensed this was the beginning of the end of their exclusive domain over the Territory. The Indians asked for more time to consider the conditions Cooley presented.

After twelve days, Cooley sent the Indians home and told them he would negotiate with individual delegations later. In the following spring, he made treaties in Washington with each of the Five Civilized Tribes. These became known as the Treaties of 1866. They represented another milestone in Oklahoma history because they included provisions that the Seminoles sell all their lands to the United States for fifteen cents per acre and the Creeks cede the western half of their lands for thirty cents an acre. The Seminoles in turn purchased another two hundred thousand-acre tract for their new home. The Creek and Seminole lands ceded to the government became the center of a long struggle and eventually the first lands in Oklahoma opened to white settlement.

The Fort Smith Council brought about the first meeting between two men who were to have great impact on Oklahoma history. Milton W. Reynolds, valedictorian at the University of Michigan in 1856, had come West to be a part of the exciting frontier. Starting in 1859 in Nebraska City, he founded and edited newspapers in frontier towns of Nebraska and Kansas. While traveling through the Indian Territory on horseback in 1869, he was overwhelmed at the beauty of the land and devoted most of his life until 1889

seeking the opening of the Territory to non-Indian settlement in a manner that would also be just to the tribes. He covered the Fort Smith Council for the New York *Tribune* and his own newspaper, the *Lawrence Kansas State Journal*.

The other young man was Elias C. Boudinot, whose father was assassinated after signing the New Echota Treaty of 1835 that traded Cherokee lands in Georgia for those in the new Indian Territory. Young Boudinot was a leader of the Southern Cherokee faction and a delegate to the Council. He was a persuasive orator and an opportunist. Reynolds and Boudinot were the real pioneers in the long struggle to open the Oklahoma lands to non-Indian settlement.

While attending the great Medicine Lodge Council in 1867, Milton W. Reynolds was attacked by Black Kettle, a Cheyenne chief. Kicking Bird, a Kiowa chief, saved his life and Reynolds adopted the pen name, Kicking Bird, to show his gratitude.

No sooner had the 1866 treaties concluded in Washington than white settlers began almost a mass movement to western lands. The Homestead Act of 1862 offered 160 acres of land in the public domain to those who had not rebelled against the government. Thousands took advantage of the offer, including many Civil War veterans. Unfortunately, they invaded Indian lands as well as those in the public domain. The first intrusions were on the Indian lands in Kansas, but many settlers also looked longingly at the Indian Territory. Stories told by travelers of the Territory's richness and beauty had created a mystique about the land.

In August 1871, Boudinot aroused settlers' interest in the Oklahoma Territory lands. By this time he had joined the Katy Railroad organization of Robert M. Stevens in Parsons, Kansas. Also in this frontier town was Milton W. Reynolds, now owner of the *Parsons Sun*. Boudinot published, in the *Sun* and the *Lawrence Journal*, the first public statement that the Creek and Seminole lands sold to the government were subject to homesteading. When the United States bought the lands, there were no conditions to the title, Boudinot said. He wrote:

> The title is absolute...it is public land...the Indian title being entirely extinguished it is as much a portion of the public domain as any other organized territory.

Since the Oklahoma lands were public domain, Boudinot contended that any settler had a right to homestead on them. Reynolds published thousands of copies of the *Sun* and scattered them all over the frontier and in Washington. By November, Boudinot's claim had inspired more than five hundred settlers to move into Oklahoma. They were immediately evicted on orders of William W. Belknap, secretary of war. Reynolds disagreed with Boudinot. Rather than through invasions, he believed the only legal way to open the Territory was through Congress, and he urged Congress to act quickly. He predicted the settlers would keep invading the territory and there would not be enough soldiers to keep them out.

His prediction was correct. Unorganized efforts to settle in Oklahoma continued. Then, in 1879, Boudinot repeated his assertion that Oklahoma lands were public domain and anybody had a right to settle on them. This time his letter appeared in the Chicago *Times*. His words made "On to Oklahoma" a rallying cry for homesteaders.

Up to now, the settlers had formed colonies in southern Kansas, but Boudinot's claims caused hundreds to flock into the Oklahoma Territory. The most publicized actions were those of Charles C. Carpenter in the spring of 1879. With the backing of Independence, Kansas businessmen, Carpenter egged the settlers on. He taunted Pres. Rutherford B. Hayes' proclamation that the Indian lands were not open to settlement and intruders would be thrown out. But when the government called his bluff, he disappeared, leaving his followers disappointed and leaderless.

Suddenly, in the late fall of 1879, the colonization effort took on new life as Capt. David L. Payne, Civil War veteran, Indian fighter, and frontiersman, arrived in southern Kansas and began organizing his Oklahoma Colony. At forty-three, Payne was a colorful figure, tall, broad-shouldered, and persuasive. Some compared him with his second cousin, Davy Crockett, as he strode through frontier settlements wearing a broad-brimmed hat and boots. Payne quickly recruited membership in his colony and collected an estimated one hundred thousand dollars. There is little doubt that railroads, especially the Katy and Frisco, were helping him. They, too, wanted Oklahoma opened to settlement.

On a visit to Wichita, Payne attracted the attention of William L. Couch, whose family had emigrated from North Carolina. Couch had operated a grain elevator in Wichita, and in 1879 was dealing in livestock. He had several times traveled over cattle trails through the Indian Territory. He listened to Payne's appeal, then sent his wife to live with his parents and joined Payne. Payne's assortment of farmers, businessmen, craftsmen, and homesteaders became known as the Boomers.

In April 1880, Payne, followed by a caravan of covered wagons, led his first expedition into the Oklahoma land in defiance of the government. He was arrested and his followers were escorted back to Kansas. The venture made him a hero and his membership grew. From then until 1885, the Boomers ventured into the Oklahoma Territory at least fifteen times, often traveling during winter months. They forded icy streams and crossed frozen rivers and creeks. During bitterly cold nights they huddled in their covered wagons and some men slept outdoors around campfires. They took their wives and children with them and enough implements and supplies to make a living from the soil for, on each excursion, they dreamed of staying in the new land.

In June 1883, after he led a group of Boomers into the Cherokee Outlet in northern Oklahoma, Payne was arrested again. His followers were sent back to Kansas but Payne and his leaders were held for a month. They were subjected to harsh treatment and virtually dragged to Fort Smith for a trial. When they were finally freed, Payne was welcomed as a martyr and hero as he returned to Kansas.

The Boomers staged celebrations all along the frontier when, on November 20, 1884, Judge Cassius G. Foster of the district court of Kansas ruled the Boomers' efforts to colonize Oklahoma did not show a conspiracy to commit an offense against the United States. He dismissed all charges against Payne. The Boomers interpreted Foster's ruling as meaning that Oklahoma lands were in public domain and that any citizen could settle there. Their joy turned to sadness on November 27, 1884, when Payne collapsed while eating breakfast in Wellington and died about an hour later.

Payne was succeeded by William L. Couch, vice-president of the colony, and Payne's right-hand man. Although not as flamboyant as Payne, Couch was very capable and commanded the Boomers' respect. He was as unyielding as Payne on the status of Oklahoma lands, and he had become an authority on federal laws relating to homesteading.

Couch immediately rallied the Boomers and within ten days he entered Oklahoma with a party of two hundred settlers. This expedition is often considered the beginning of Stillwater history. On December 12, the Boomers camped on the banks of a stream they called Stillwater Creek. There they decided to make their homes. Their route to the site became known as Payne's Trail and their encampment was called Camp Stillwater. They built homes, dugouts, and other shelters.

Their presence was soon challenged. On Wednesday, Christmas Eve, 1884, Lieutenant M. W. Day and his cavalry troops arrived to arrest Couch. The government had decided to ignore Judge Foster's ruling. The armed troops lined up and faced the Boomers, many of whom were watching from dugouts, rifles in hand. Couch stood in the foreground holding his Winchester. Day ordered Couch to surrender or be shot down, but Couch refused and said the Boomers would return the fire. Day told five of his men to tie Couch but rescinded the order as Couch raised his rifle. Day knew he lacked manpower to overwhelm the Boomers, so he agreed to wait overnight before pressing the matter.

Day wired for reinforcements on Christmas day. He said a great slaughter would result if his thirty-nine men attacked Couch's estimated two hundred Boomers. In his dispatch, Day made the first recorded reference to the name of the settlement. "The settlers call this place the town of Stillwater," he wrote. "It is about three miles below the crossing of the Stillwater by the Arkansas City (B. & M.) road." From Fort Reno, Maj. Thomas B. Dewees forwarded the request for reinforcements to army headquarters in Missouri and added, "The Mr. Couch named as President of the Colony is an old offender."

Couch also went into action. He wired Pres. Chester A. Arthur, urging him to stay the use of troops. He said his people were "law abiding settlers disturbing no one and violating no law of the United States." And Couch added, "We are unwilling to submit to military arrest while under…civil law." He then gathered the settlers on the banks of Stillwater Creek and prepared a petition to Congress to open the territory to settlement. It was presented to Congress on January 7, 1895, signed by 154 settlers, including Couch, his father, Meshach H., and his brothers, Joseph and Meshach Quinton Couch.

In the petition, Couch restated the position of Elias C. Boudinot, that the Oklahoma Territory was public land purchased from the Creeks and Seminole Indians and paid for in full. The title rested now with the United States and the Boomers had a right to be there.

Meantime, the Boomers and soldiers became friends. They visited back and forth and helped one another endure the bitter weather. The banks of Stillwater Creek were glazed with ice and the soldiers suffered more than the Boomers. A doctor in the Boomer camp treated soldiers who became ill and frostbitten. The settlers and soldiers made it obvious they did not want to shoot at one another. This angered Gen. Philip Sheridan who reminded them that "the performance of duty should not be embarrassed by exhibition of sympathy for the intruders."

The petition had no immediate effects. Col. Edward M. Hatch and 350 cavalrymen arrived in late January. By this time the Boomer encampment had grown to more than 300. Hatch first warned the Boomers of the consequences of resisting the government. He then positioned troops to cut off all supplies to the settlers. His next move was to withdraw his men from the range of Boomer rifle fire but close enough to aim artillery fire at the encampment. The Boomers had no alternative but to surrender and to leave Oklahoma. Couch was imprisoned for three weeks but was released when witnesses against him failed to show up.

This was the last major Boomer expedition to Oklahoma, although Couch took a smaller group to near present day Oklahoma City later in 1885. Couch knew the time had come to change tactics. While the Boomers had been invading the Territory, the struggle had made headway on other fronts.

Sensing the climax of the Oklahoma movement was near, Milton W. Reynolds had sent thousands of copies of his newspaper to members of Congress, public officials, and settlers who wanted to come West. He had become recognized as an expert on Indian affairs. Some of his analytical articles were five thousand words in length. He also organized delegations to push the cause in Washington and went to the nation's capital himself to help agitate Congressional action.

Congressmen James B. Weaver of Iowa, Charles H. Mansur of Missouri, William Springer of Illinois, and Bishop W. Perkins of Kansas were also pushing for a bill to open the Territory to white settlement. Couch, Col. Sam Crocker, and other Boomers put on civilian clothing and went to Washington. The Boomer movement had made the nation aware of the problems of homesteaders and Indians. It had aroused the sympathy of many Americans. The climax of the struggle was near.

Victory finally came in 1889. A bill by Springer passed the House of Representatives on February 1. The Senate balked at first but finally yielded when the House attached a rider to the Indian Appropriation Bill, which had already passed the Senate. The Bill opening Oklahoma to settlement passed in time for Pres. Grover Cleveland to sign it just before his term expired March 3, 1889. On March 23, Pres. Benjamin Harrison signed a proclamation that the Oklahoma lands would be opened for settlement on April 22, 1889. With this, the first town in the Territory, Stillwater, Oklahoma, would come to life again.

Milton W. Reynolds, frontier journalist
and legislator, fanned the flames of the
Oklahoma movement with stories written
under the nom de plum *Kicking Bird.* He
made Oklahoma known nationally as
"*Land of the Fair God.*" Reynolds disagreed with the Boomers and Elias C.
Boudinot. He believed only Congress could
open Oklahoma to settlement.
*Courtesy of the Archives and Manuscripts
Division, Oklahoma Historical Society*

After the Indians ceded their lands to the
government in the Treaties of 1866, the
Indian Territory became two territories
instead of one. When the Indians were
asked what they wanted to call the new
territory, Rev. Allen Wright, a well-
educated Choctaw leader and minister,
replied "Oklahoma." The name was
derived from two Choctaw words, "okla,"
(people), and "humma or homma," (red).
Wright intended the translation to be
"Territory of Red People."
*Courtesy of the Archives and Manuscripts
Division, Oklahoma Historical Society*

A friend of both David L. Payne and Milton W. Reynolds, Elias C. Boudinot aroused settlers with his claims that the Oklahoma Territory was public land and anyone had a right to settle there. The Boomers used his argument to justify their invasions of the Territory. Boudinot was accused by some Cherokees of betraying the Indians and promoting the Oklahoma movement for selfish reasons. Even today, he is a controversial historical figure. Courtesy of the Archives and Manuscripts Division, Oklahoma Historical Society

Sometimes called "Oklahoma's Moses" and "the Father of Oklahoma," David Lewis Payne donned coat and tie for his roles as Kansas legislator and assistant doorkeeper of the United States House of Representatives. From the time Stillwater was settled in 1889, there was little doubt the county would be named for him. Courtesy of the Kansas State Historical Society

As hundreds of the land hungry responded to his appeal to join his Oklahoma colony, David L. Payne led them in a series of invasions into the Oklahoma Territory. Pictured here is one of the first. Payne was well acquainted with Elias C. Boudinot, and he based his actions on Boudinot's contentions that the Oklahoma lands were public lands and subject to settlement. Courtesy of the Archives and Manuscripts Division, Oklahoma Historical Society

*These seven men were the "brain trust" or strategists of the Boomer movement. Front row from left are A. C. McCord, secretary, David L. Payne, president, William L. Couch, vice-president of the Oklahoma Colony, and Joe Pugsley. Back row are H. H. Stafford, surveyor, G. F. Goodrich, and A. P. Lewis.
Courtesy of the Archives and Manuscripts Division, Oklahoma Historical Society*

David L. Payne, center in top hat, leads a group of Boomers across the Kansas line in 1883. This was one of his last invasions of the Oklahoma Territory before he died

It was at this Boomer camp on the North Canadian River that U.S. Army troops arrested David L. Payne in 1883. He and his followers suffered greatly as they were virtually dragged to the Texas line and then to Fort Smith for trial.
Courtesy of the Kansas State Historical Society

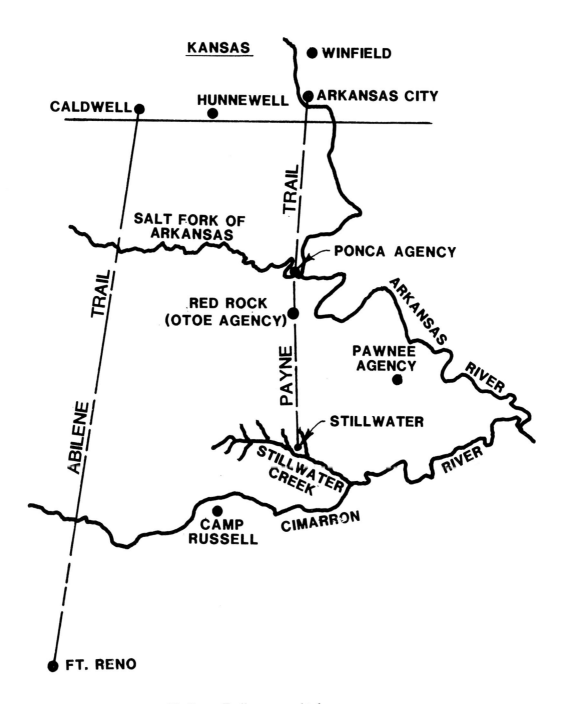

KANSAS ● WINFIELD

CALDWELL ● HUNNEWELL ● ARKANSAS CITY

TRAIL

SALT FORK OF
ARKANSAS

TRAIL

PONCA AGENCY

ARKANSAS

RED ROCK
(OTOE AGENCY) ●

PAYNE

PAWNEE
AGENCY ●

RIVER

ABILENE

STILLWATER

STILLWATER
CREEK

RIVER

CAMP
RUSSELL ●

CIMARRON

● FT. RENO

*The Payne Trail was named to honor
David L. Payne after his death in November 1884. It was this route that William L.
Couch followed to the Stillwater Valley,
where he made his stand against the U.S.
Cavalry. The trail was said to be Payne's
favorite route into the Territory and he
plowed furrows along the way as markers.
Map courtesy of Dr. B. B. Chapman, from
his book,* The Founding of Stillwater,
drawn by Dwight Zimbelman

Meshach and Mary Bryan Couch, parents of William L. Couch, vigorously supported their son in his efforts to open Oklahoma to settlement. Some said Meshach was a powerful force in the Boomer movement. He was in the 1884 settlement on Stillwater Creek. Meshach and Mary settled in Oklahoma City after the 1889 Land Rush. Courtesy of Edna M. Couch, granddaughter of William L. Couch

William L. Couch was fifteen when he took over the family farm in the mountains of North Carolina after his father, Meshach, volunteered for the Union Army. William slipped through the forest at night carrying food to his father, who hid in caves while making his way through the Confederate lines. The bitterness toward him for siding with the North caused Meshach to emigrate to Kansas in 1866 with his wife and six children.
Courtesy of Edna M. Couch, grand-daughter of William L. Couch

William Lewis Couch was thirty-four when he succeeded David L. Payne as leader of the Boomers and led them to the Stillwater Valley. This picture was taken about that time.
Courtesy of Edna M. Couch, grand-daughter of William L. Couch

In March 1884, Mathias W. Day was commissioned a lieutenant in the U.S. Army. In December he faced the most difficult decision of his career as he was ordered to evict William L. Couch's Boomer colony from the banks of Stillwater Creek. When bloodshed seemed imminent, he wisely retreated and wired for reinforcements. "The settlers call this place the town of Stillwater," he stated in the wire. It was the first recorded reference to the town, its name, and the name of Stillwater Creek. The army succeeded in its mission by cutting off the Boomers' supply lines. Courtesy of the Oklahoma State University Library, Special Collections

One of the earliest references to Stillwater, Oklahoma, is on this certificate dated January 2, 1885, entitling Edward F. Wilcox to 160 acres of land. The certificate was made out by H. H. Stafford, surveyor of the colony, and signed by W. (William) L. Couch. Courtesy of Edna M. Couch, granddaughter of William L. Couch

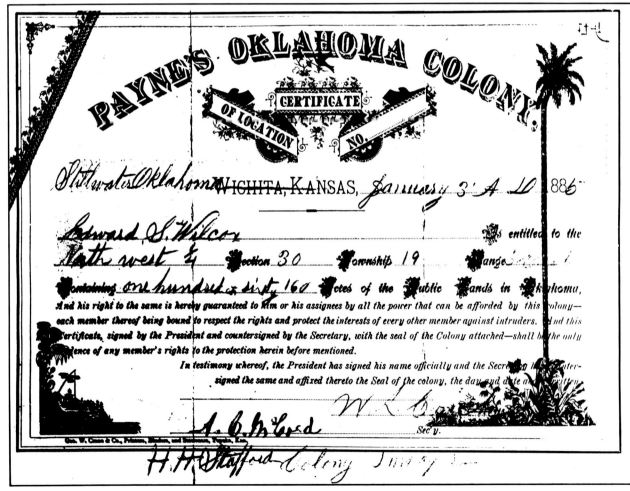

A Boomer encampment in the Oklahoma Territory shows an early version of a travel trailer. The covered wagons carried bedding, cooking utensils, clothes lines, clothes, washing equipment, folded tents, and a food supply.
Courtesy of the Archives and Manuscripts Division, Oklahoma Historical Society

Bishop W. Perkins of Kansas was, according to Milton Reynolds, the man who forced the U.S. Senate to pass the Oklahoma Bill by attaching a rider to the Indian Appropriations Bill. The town of Perkins was named for him in December 1889 after he helped establish a star route mail line from Perkins to Mulhall, the nearest railroad stop.
Courtesy of the Kansas State Historical Society

51

Chapter 5

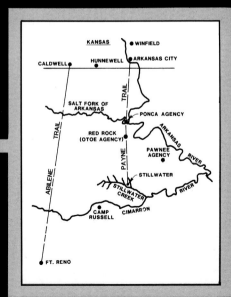

KANSAS WINFIELD

CALDWELL HUNNEWELL ARKANSAS CITY

TRAIL

SALT FORK OF ARKANSAS

PONCA AGENCY

RED ROCK (OTOE AGENCY)

PAWNEE AGENCY

ARKANSAS RIVER

PAYNE

STILLWATER

STILLWATER CREEK

RIVER

ABILENE

TRAIL

CAMP RUSSELL

CIMARRON

FT. RENO

STILLWATER—"HERE TO STAY"

In late March 1889, John H. Barnes and Robert A. Lowry excitedly rushed into the general store of Will and Ambrose Swiler in Angus, Iowa. Lowry carried a copy of President Harrison's proclamation opening Oklahoma to settlement on April 22, 1889. After some discussion, all four decided to pull up stakes and seek a new life in Oklahoma. Angus, a small mining town of five thousand, was declining rapidly.

"But we'll have to leave immediately," Lowry said. "The Run is on April 2." He had misread the proclamation. He and Barnes hastily packed a tent and a few necessities and headed for southern Kansas. Lowry told his wife and three children he would send for them soon. The Swiler brothers could not move so quickly but promised to follow later. Only when Lowry and Barnes reached Kansas City did they learn of their error. They arrived in Arkansas City on April 2.

They were astonished to find that hundreds of settlers had already arrived at the Kansas border. Some had for years dreamed of a new home in the fabled Indian Territory. They streamed to the area in covered wagons, buggies, horseback, and on foot. Even couples in their eighties wanted a chance in the new land.

Not all of Oklahoma was opened to settlement in 1889—only lands in the center of the Territory ceded by the Seminoles and Creeks in 1866. These had become known as the Unassigned Lands and consisted largely of the area now made up of Payne, Logan, Kingfisher, Oklahoma, Canadian, and Cleveland Counties. The government had divided the land into 11,000 sections of 160 acres each. A homesteader could stake a claim to one section but he must establish a home and reside on it within six months and cultivate it for five years. A half-section of land could be set aside for a townsite.

The homesteaders along the Kansas border were upset because on the day of the land run they would have to travel through the Cherokee Outlet before they could enter the Unassigned Lands and stake their claims. This would be a fifty-eight mile journey and place them at a great disadvantage to settlers who were waiting to rush for claims on the southern, eastern, and western borders of the Unassigned Lands.

Lowry was one of a delegation that protested to Capt. Jack Hays, cavalry commander. Hays agreed and immediately wired Washington. The next morning permission came for the settlers to proceed through the Outlet to the Oklahoma Territory line.

The land seekers all along the twenty-five-mile-long encampment immediately prepared for the journey, which would start the next morning, April 18. Lowry and Barnes bought two unbroken fast ponies, which they thought might give them an advantage during the run. Lowry's mount, with him in the saddle, immediately plunged off a bridge into a fifteen-foot-deep water hole of the Walnut River.

Barnes and Lowry had divided camp duties and Lowry, the cook, suggested that Barnes do the laundry before the trip. After watching women in an adjacent wagon boil clothes in a kettle, Barnes asked to borrow their facility. The women giggled as Barnes placed his and Lowry's clothes in the boiling water. He had included his own red longhandles. Lowry was furious when Barnes sheepishly handed him his underwear, shirts, and jeans, now all a glowing red. He breathed a sigh of relief as Lowry angrily shouted, "Don't you ever touch anything of mine again." The two were conspicuous in their red attire the rest of the journey.

A driving rain came that night and the wind shifted to the north. Many of the settlers were soaked and cold as they began the trip through the Outlet. It was 10:00 A.M. before the caravan started moving, to the cheers of several hundred spectators who had come from Arkansas City and other towns to see the spectacle.

The rains had softened the prairie soil, and the covered wagons turned it into a sea of mud. The caravan crept fifteen miles the first day. Lowry and Barnes let a settler drive their wagon while they rode ahead on their ponies. Lowry, a good marksman, shot enough quail, prairie chicken, and plover for meals. When he returned, Barnes had a fire ready and did the cooking. Most of the settlers had loaded their wagon with kindling before leaving Kansas.

Not far from Barnes and Lowry another man camped alone in a wooded area. Louis J. Jardot, twenty-seven, had come from Limeridge, Wisconsin, to find a new life in the Oklahoma Territory. He was frying bacon that evening when he looked up and was startled to find a group of Indians in a circle around him. They motioned him to remove his skillet from the fire and to mount his pony. They led him over a hill to a field where other Indians were stripping meat from cattle they had slaughtered. They motioned for Jardot to take some of the meat. It was their gesture of hospitality. Jardot took a sliver of beef and hurried back to his campsite.

On the afternoon of the second day, the caravan reached the Ponca Indian agency on the banks of Salt Fork River south of present day Ponca City. Rain had sent the Salt Fork over its banks. Captain Hays ordered two rail cars of lumber sent to a railroad bridge that crossed the river and told the settlers they could cross the next morning. Some tried to cross in the night by the light of a big bonfire. Their wagons washed away and their horses drowned, but the people were finally rescued. Down stream, Indians set up a successful ferry by stretching a cable across the river tied to trees on each side. They charged $2.50 per family. The Indians braved the swift current to rescue several homesteaders who tried to make it on their own.

On the next evening near sundown, the travelers reached the top of a ridge just north of present-day Stillwater. As they watched, the clouds suddenly rolled away and the Stillwater Valley came in full view. The homesteaders could see for several miles as most of the land was rolling prairie and only a few trees along small streams dotted the landscape.

This land would be their future home. This would be Stillwater. Some homesteaders gasped, others cheered, and some shed tears as they gazed on the landscape. Robert A. Lowry was a lawyer, but his description of the scene was poetic:

In front of the settlers as far as the eye could see was the rolling variegated green expanse, the trees in full leaf, the spring grass tall enough to wave in the wind and the hillside decked with prairie flowers. There were parks of jack oak and post oak on the hills, the dark green of the timber that fringed the winding streams between. A poet described it as "A jewel in nature's open hand."

Lowry and Barnes decided to explore closer to the line from which the land run would be made. A half mile south they saw a man camped under a large tree. Barnes described him as "an elderly man." He was forty-seven. He smiled and beckoned them to join him. "I'm George Gardenhire," he said, and invited Barnes and Lowry to share his fire and food. They camped there that night. It was this simple set of circumstances that brought together men who were to have great impact on the future of a new frontier town.

That night they took turns guarding the horses. A number of land-seekers had made the trip by hitching rides from others. Now they were stealing horses for the big land run. Some were slipping across the line at night to beat the rush. These were the Sooners.

The historic day of the Land Run, Monday, April 22, 1889, dawned bright and clear. Campfires burned all through the encampments as homesteaders packed their wagons and cooked enough food to last the rest of the day. Lowry and Barnes were joined by a Boomer named Chayne from Couch's 1884 encampment. He knew the land well, and they invited him to lead them. The largest camp of settlers was on Cow Creek on the western edge of present Stillwater. Further west was a camp on Stillwater Creek, and to the east the land hungry had gathered on Boomer Creek. On Chayne's advice, the three moved further east to due north of the present Fairlawn Cemetery.

At mid-morning, Lowry and Barnes checked with Captain Hays and set their watches. Tension grew as covered wagons, spring wagons, and men and women mounted on horses gathered at the line. At exactly noon, an army sergeant pointed a gun skyward, shouted "Let'er go Gallagher!" and fired. The story of the land run has been told many times, but Robert A. Lowry's account of the rush to the Stillwater Valley was especially dramatic:

The settlement of the territory comprising Payne County began when the guns were fired. Men on foot leaped across the line and drove a stake. Men on horseback applied quirt and spur and shot to the front. Men with teams, buggies, and wagons plied whip, and the crowd was off....Those with fast horses and good teams set their eyes on the bottom lands along Stillwater Creek and the Cimarron River. Those less qualified for the long race and the hard pace, took what they could get.

Lowry and Barnes went a short distance south, then veered west across Boomer Creek. Lowry staked a claim in the area of present day Lowry Street. Barnes went south of there to a point on Stillwater Creek near Thirteenth Street. Lowry recorded that, within one hour, the Valley had been settled.

Fortunately for the new homesteaders, Monday night, April 22, 1889, was clear, bright, and warm. They cooked their meals over campfires and slept on the prairie grass beneath the stars. Many had left their wagons behind and ridden horses to their claims. Some made the run on foot.

In each camp, family members took turns standing guard as roving bands of squatters still looking for claims sought to take over land from legitimate claim holders. Other settlers encountered Sooners who had slipped across the line early. Some Sooners were special deputies assigned to catch other Sooners but as the run began, they threw away their badges and staked claims for themselves.

Among those who encountered trouble was Louis J. Jardot. Scarcely had he staked his claim and unpacked his bedroll than two men rode up and dismounted. One flung a small axe toward him that stuck in the ground at his feet. The other pointed a shotgun at him and ordered him off the land. Jardot had a few minutes earlier given his gun to a family in a covered wagon. He had no alternative but to leave. But as he rode away, his anger grew. He pursued the covered wagon and retrieved his gun. A short time later he returned to his claim and surprised the claim jumpers. They left and never returned.

The settlers found few remnants of William L. Couch's Boomer colony of 1884. The forty dugouts and log huts had largely collapsed and were covered with vines. John Barnes discovered a row of six log cabins the Boomers had built along what is now South Main near Thirteenth Street. The cavalry had set fire to them. The roofs were burned and the sides badly damaged. Of those in the 1884 Couch camp, only six returned for the Run of 1889 to Stillwater Creek. As one of them, Chayne, rode by, Barnes waved at him and said, "Well, we made it," and Chayne yelled back. "Yes, and this time we're here to stay."

The man called the "Father of Stillwater" by the first settlers was Robert Arnold Lowry. He staked his claim a few minutes after the land run in 1889. He donated eighty acres of it to secure the townsite, planned the town layout, became first postmaster, a member of the first town council, and led the fight to bring the county seat and Oklahoma A&M College to Stillwater. Born in Oswego, Illinois, on September 24, 1859, he later worked his way through Iowa State University and the Iowa University law school. He practiced law and became mayor of Angus, Iowa. Excited by the potential of the Oklahoma Territory, he made the run to the Stillwater Valley. He died on March 6, 1920.
Courtesy of the NewsPress

John H. Barnes was twenty-eight when he and his closest friend, Robert A. Lowry, traveled from Iowa to the Stillwater Valley in 1889. The first store and post office were located on his property. He was a member of the company to locate a townsite and his homestead near Stillwater Creek was one site considered.
Courtesy of Barbara Hartley Dunn and Mrs. C. E. (Ruth) Donart

As future Stillwater residents began the trek across the Cherokee Outlet, Robert A. Lowry described the scene: "The winding cattle trails to the territory being opened were moving, weaving ribbons of white-topped prairie schooners, flanked and followed by troops of horsemen." Four thousand schooners were in the caravan and hundreds of citizens stood watching the historic scene.
Courtesy of the Western History Collection, University of Oklahoma

5th U.S. CAVALRY. Co's D AND L [...] AT. OKLAHOMA. April 1st 1889

To keep order among the settlers' camps that extended almost as a solid line from Arkansas City to Caldwell, Kansas, the Fifth U.S. Cavalry arrived on April 1, 1889. After assisting the homesteaders across the Cherokee Outlet from April 18 to April 21, they positioned themselves along the Oklahoma Territory line for the great Land Run of 1889.
Courtesy of the Archives and Manuscripts Division, Oklahoma Historical Society

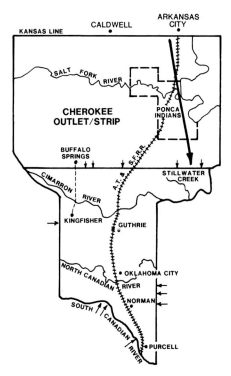

When the government gave homesteaders permission to move across the Cherokee Outlet to make the Run of 1889, they traveled this route from near Arkansas City to the border of the Unassigned Lands. Arrows show principal points from which the run was made. On the day of the run, those heading for the Stillwater Valley were only three miles from what would be the new townsite. That point is now in the city limits. Other settlers took the A.T. & S.F. trains, especially to Guthrie. A stage line then reached from Buffalo Springs, Kansas, to Kingfisher, Oklahoma.
Map by Dwight Zimbelman

A native of Belfort, France, Louis J. Jardot came with his parents to the U.S. when he was twelve. During the Land Run of 1889, he homesteaded 160 acres at the southeast corner of what is now Western and Twelfth streets. Although best remembered for the Opera House, he established the first brick yard in this section of Oklahoma and built many Stillwater structures, including Alcott School, Norwood School, the Linden Hotel, and other business buildings. Three generations of Jardots were known for skilled craftsmanship in brick laying and masonry.
Courtesy of Mr. and Mrs. Harold Jardot

After the land hungry struggled across the Cherokee Outlet, they gathered all along the Oklahoma Territory line waiting for the signal that would send them rushing for homesteads. The only lands opened April 22, 1889, were those in central Oklahoma ceded by Indian tribes in the Treaties of 1866.
Courtesy of the Archives and Manuscripts Division, Oklahoma Historical Society

Fighting A Contest

After the Land Run, homesteaders set up tents on their claims and stood guard through the night to fight off claim jumpers, some of whom were armed. Settlers who had no tents slept on the grass. Many had no food, but they clung to their claims.
Courtesy of the Archives and Manuscripts Division, Oklahoma Historical Society

When Oklahoma was finally opened to settlement, William L. Couch chose not to return to the Stillwater Valley. He moved on to what the A. T. & S.F. railroad called Oklahoma Station, later Oklahoma City, where he became the first mayor. He is shown here in the foreground with Bull Bear, a Cheyenne chief, who attended an Indian conference there.
Courtesy of Edna M. Couch, granddaughter of William L. Couch

George Clark, center, built a sod house on his claim about five miles south of Stillwater just after the 1889 Land Run. The small community of Otego sprung up near there about three miles south of Payne Center off present Husband Street. Otego had a blacksmith shop, general store, and a post office from April 19, 1894, until September 30, 1903. It was named for a small Kansas community that had been the previous home of one of the settlers.
Courtesy of the Sheerar Museum, Skinner Family Collection

Alfred M. Daugherty was one of Stillwater's first lawyers. His cabin was on his homestead south of Ingalls after the 1889 land run, but he spent most of his time practicing law in the Stillwater Hotel. His son, Royal, who lived in the cabin as a boy, returned years later and posed with his wife for this picture. A. W. Daugherty and Art Daugherty, grandson and great-grandson of Alfred are among four Daugherty generations who still live in Stillwater but the family no longer owns the homestead. Courtesy of Art Daugherty, Jr.

*Joe King built this home at 1113 South Main after the 1889 Land Run. It has been replaced by a brick building. In the background is a glimpse of part of the Orlando M. Eyler home on the left in the early days.
Courtesy of the H. E. Ricker family*

Chapter
6

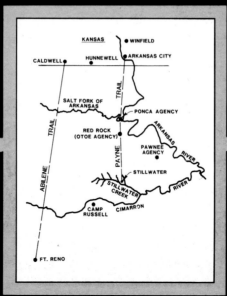

THE EARLY YEARS

In spite of hardships the settlers endured on the trail to the Stillwater Valley, their struggle was only beginning. Even as the village of three hundred took form, its leaders were emerging and had already proclaimed they would make Stillwater the best city in northeastern Oklahoma.

Some of these who would shape Stillwater's future were very young. Two attorneys, Frank J. Wikoff and Frank Hutto, were twenty-two and twenty-six, respectively. Harry B. Bullen was twenty-three and Seth (Hays) Hamilton, twenty-six. Robert A. Lowry was twenty-nine and Louis Jardot, twenty-eight. Orlando M. Eyler and Will Swiler were in their mid-thirties. Among those considered in the older generation were Amon W. Swope, forty-six, and James S. Hunt, the first county clerk, fifty-six. Richard B. Foster, the first pastor of the Congregational Church and the first county superintendent of schools was an incredible sixty-four.

Stillwater owes a deep debt of gratitude to its pioneers. They had the foresight to see what it would take to lay the foundation for a great city of the future. They fought with courage and determination to win every important battle. Their first big fight came sooner than expected. A site had to be found for the business district and the city government. Everybody knew the town would be called Stillwater, but where to put it brought about a great legal fight.

To pick a townsite, the settlers on May 15, 1889, formally organized the Stillwater Town Company. Its stockholders included 119 pioneers. Since no towns were nearby, the Town Company members went to Winfield, Kansas, and organized under Kansas laws. They elected William J. Hodges president. The company chose a committee to lay out a townsite in the Stillwater Creek areas. Their most specific instruction was to choose a townsite at the mouth of Stillwater Creek where it empties into the Cimarron River. This was eleven miles from its present location.

Some of the members had different ideas, including Hodges, who had established a claim on Stillwater Creek three miles west of town. He wanted the townsite there and he had influenced some members to agree with him. The committee traveled back to the Stillwater area with two prairie schooners, three saddle horses, and camp equipment. They first studied the Hodges site, then moved east

and established a camp at Cap Nipp's Crossing where Cow Creek empties into Stillwater Creek on the western edge of present Stillwater. The crossing and cattle trail were named for Captain J. B. Nipp, of Cowley County, Kansas, who had settled on a ranch near Wild Horse Creek.

The next day the committee explored the Cap Nipp crossing as a possible townsite, then journeyed east to the claim of John H. Barnes. From there it went to the site of Capt. William L. Couch's 1884 Boomer camp near where Boomer Creek empties into Stillwater Creek. There the men reached one conclusion: they were not going eleven miles further to the mouth of Stillwater Creek. It was just too far. This eliminated the banks of the Cimarron River as a townsite.

While they werre pondering what to do, Lewis Cooper, a member of the Town Company, brought astonishing news. He had learned of an unclaimed eighty-acre tract in the heart of the area. It bordered on the claims of Barnes, Lowry, David Husband, Sanford Duncan, and Frank E. Duck. How this could have happened remains a mystery one hundred years later. The committee made a quick trip to the site. They seemed to know instinctively this was where they wanted Stillwater to be. To make sure the site didn't escape them, they chose a committee member, Garnett Burks, to stake a claim on it and file it quickly with the understanding that he was doing this to preserve a townsite. This was on May 22, 1889. The Town Company was overjoyed.

The company members received a second shock on August 10. While a group of them were looking over their prize site, they found a carpenter erecting a building. He treated them as intruders. And on that day Burks wrote to the Commissioner of the General Land Office: "...my carpenter was stopped by a Party of men claiming to belong to a town company known as Stillwater Townsite....I located on that land before there was ever any town...." Garnett Burks was claiming for himself the beautiful site the company had chosen for Stillwater. Thus began a legal fight that lasted until mid-1891.

The Stillwater pioneers did not wait for a legal decision on the land. They proceeded to immediately get the town established. Robert A. Lowry donated 80 acres; Sanford Duncan and David Husband each donated 40 acres to make the townsite total 240 acres, counting the Burks claim. Otto Weile, the surveyor, platted the town, using Winfield as a pattern. The land Burks claimed extended from Ninth Street to seventy feet north of Sixth just west of present-day Husband Street. Westward it reached from the courthouse lot to Washington Street. The east part of it was divided into lots. Lowry gave the eighty acres on the condition that Main Street be located on his land, otherwise Main might have been a block west of its present location.

With such details accomplished, June 11, 1889, became a big day in Stillwater history. Townspeople began gathering early that day for the first event—the drawing for town lots. Each member of the town company was entitled to one business lot and two residential lots, each 25 by 40 feet. George Madden brought gun wads from Winfield and wrote lot numbers on them. He brought a wagon to the center of the eight hundred block of South Main to use for a platform. Madden placed the gun wads into two hats, one for business lots and one for residential lots. A boy drew the wads from the hat as each town company member's name was called.

In early afternoon, while the drawing was still in progress, a group of settlers organized a city government and elected its first officers. Dr. J. G. Evans was chosen mayor, although he served for only a day before deciding to return to Winfield. Madden was chosen city clerk, and T. W. Myton, treasurer. Lowry was elected president of the city council. Frank J. Wikoff was assigned the task of preparing Stillwater's city charter. In August, he became the town's first elected city attorney. The charter was adopted August 24, 1889.

Some streets were also named on June 11, including Lowry, Lewis, Husband, Duncan, Duck, and West; lots were set aside for a courthouse, the first school, and for churches.

It is probably appropriate to state here the town's pioneers were not always one big happy family. While they stood united in the effort to get the townsite back from Garnett Burks, they fought each other over possession of town lots. Lot jumping became so flagrant the council passed an ordinance to protect legitimate claimants.

At the drawing for town lots, John H. Barnes had been awarded the lot at the northwest corner of Eighth and Main. He built a foundation and walls of a building, where he intended to operate as a tinsmith. One day when he was out of town, John V. Hodges tore down the building, erected one of his own, and claimed the lot. He said Barnes had no right to it as he lived out of the city. The area from Twelfth to Fourteenth Street on South Main was considered far out then. Barnes finally won the dispute.

David Husband, a native of Wales, had forsaken his country to be a part of the American West. He joined the Boomers and was in Couch's 1884 Stillwater colony. He returned in 1889 and staked a claim just north of Lowry's property. On August 16, 1889, Orin U. Wittum accused him of being a Sooner. He said Husband was on the land the day before the run. Husband had just donated forty acres of his claim to the townsite. Wittum took the rest of it from him in the lawsuit, but sold eleven acres back to him.

On October 23, 1889, John Barnes and Ambrose Swiler armed themselves with a crowbar and hoe and went to do battle for a lot claimed by Mrs. Will Swiler on which Thomas J. Heuston was building a house. Mayor John H. Clark intervened and persuaded them to take the battle to the courts. Mrs. Swiler won her lot. Even Barnes and Robert Lowry were once accused of being Sooners.

In August 1890, the people of Stillwater decided to have a showdown with Garnett Burks over rights to the townsite. More than one hundred of them signed an application for a townsite that was immediately filed with the Register of the Guthrie Land Office, because of the fuss over David Husband's land and Burk's claims, the application was rejected and a hearing was ordered by the commissioner of the General Land Office.

The legal battle lasted for more than six months. The townspeople said Burks had betrayed them by claiming the land, that he had established no residence there, and had made no improvements. Burks claimed he had legally filed for the land as his own from the beginning. He said the reason there were no improvements was that the Town Company members kept tearing them down and throwing them off the property. Finally, on March 14, 1891, Secretary of the Interior John W. Noble ruled that Burks did not make his homestead entry in good faith. He said it must be canceled. The people celebrated the victory. Not only were they here to stay, but so was the townsite. With that matter settled, the pioneers set about in earnest to build their new town.

William J. Hodges dreamed of having the new town located on his claim three miles west of present day Stillwater. As president of the Stillwater Town Company, his influence was considerable and many assumed his land would be chosen as a townsite. His hopes were dashed when the company found eighty unclaimed acres it liked much better. Hodges later operated a feed and seed store on Main.
Courtesy of the NewsPress

Garnett Burks almost became "The Grinch Who Stole Stillwater." When the Townsite Committee found a choice eighty-acre site for the town, they asked Burks, a member, to quickly file a claim to hold it. Burks later claimed the land for himself. The committee and citizens fought back through harassment and legal action and finally regained the site on which much of central Stillwater is built.
Courtesy of Dr. B. B. Chapman

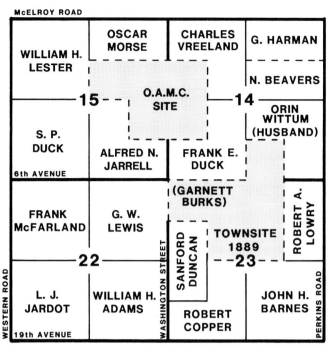

The Stillwater Townsite of 1889

The Stillwater townsite looked like this in 1889. The upper shaded area shows land provided for the OAMC site by Frank E. Duck, Charles Vreeland, Oscar M. Morse, and Alfred N. Jarrell. The center shaded area shows the townsite itself made up of the controversial claim of Garnett Burks plus land donated by Sanford Duncan, Robert A. Lowry, and David Husband. The latter's land was later taken from him by Orin Wittum in a lawsuit. Sixth Street was first known as McFarland Highway. Map by Mike Shores, courtesy of the Community Development Department, City of Stillwater

Robert A. Lowry, 'Father of Stillwater'

A powerful figure in Oklahoma politics, Robert A. Lowry was representative to the first territorial convention in Guthrie July 20, 1889. He was also a member of the Oklahoma delegation, shown here, seeking statehood in 1905. He is first on the left on the back row. Judge Thomas Doyle, who headed the statehood delegation, is on the front row, far right. In 1894, Lowry was elected to the territorial legislature where he headed the Judiciary, Ways and Means, and Criminal Jurisprudence committees. He led the fight against an effort to divide Payne County and for the retention of Oklahoma A&M College in Stillwater. In May 1900 Lowry was appointed by Territorial Governor Cassius Barnes as judge advocate on his staff with the rank of major. Lowry's status gave Stillwater great influence in territorial affairs. Courtesy of the Archives and Manuscripts Division, Oklahoma Historical Society

Robert A. Lowry and his wife, Anna, had six children and Stillwater streets are named for two of them, Fern and Chester. Lowry was a devoted father who maintained discipline mostly by a stern look. His grandson and namesake who lives in Stillwater recalled: "Sometimes he paid the children pennies to pick potato bugs in the garden or loaded them into his automobile and took them to the Lowry farm west of town." In the front row are Abigal and Ethel, and in the back, Orlo, Chester, and Theodora, five of his six children.
Courtesy of Robert A. Lowry, grandson

At age twenty-two, Frank J. Wikoff became Stillwater's first elected city attorney and wrote the city charter, which he completed in August 1889. At twenty-four he headed the committee to secure two hundred acres that would bring Oklahoma A&M College to Stillwater. Wikoff was president of the Bank of Commerce on the northwest corner of Eighth and Main streets. He later achieved statewide prominence as president of Tradesmen's National Bank in Oklahoma City and territorial bank examiner. He died August 4, 1950 in Arcadia, California.
From Portrait and Biographical Record of Oklahoma, 1910

The Stillwater Gazette.

Estd. 1889. Stillwater, Payne County, Oklahoma, Thursday, March 14, 1901. Vol. 12, No. 12

GEN. HARRISON PASSES AWAY. | MRS. NATION'S DAILY MAIL. | RACE NOW SAID TO BE OFF.

OKLAHOMA STANDARD

VOL. 1. STILLWATER, PAYNE COUNTY, OKLAHOMA, SATURDAY, AUGUST 3, 1889. NO. 1.

THE STILLWATER VALLEY

Rich, Fertile Land and a Beautiful Climate.

Plenty of Water, Grass and Heavy Timber.

Stillwater, the Metropolis of Payne County.

Not Two Months Old and Has 75 Buildings.

The Place for the Investor and Homeseeker.

The First Store in Payne County.

SWILER BROS.,

HARDWARE

STOVES, TINWARE

Blacksmith and wagon makers' supplies.

Barb wire, pumps and farm machinery.

Full line of Staple and Fancy Groceries, Flour and Feed.

South Main Street. Stillwater, I. T.

H. B. BULLEN,

LUMBER Dealer

Lath, Shingles, Doors, Windows and Mouldings.

South Main Street. Stillwater, I. T.

CLARK BROS'

RED STAR GROCERY !

All kinds of staple and fancy groceries at lowest prices.

Stillwater's first newspaper was the Oklahoma Standard. *Pictured is the front page of the first issue, August 3, 1889. Publisher Joseph Merrifield used most of the page to describe the "Beautiful" Stillwater Valley. The second newspaper was* The Stillwater Gazette, *started by Dan Murphy in December 1889.*
Courtesy of the H. E. Ricker family and the Richard F. Weilmuenster family

When the Stillwater Gazette, *founded in 1889, consolidated with the* Eagle *in 1894, the publication for a time became the* Eagle-Gazette. *The staff apparently put aside printer's aprons, scrubbed off printer's ink, and dressed up for the picture. With copy of* Eagle-Gazette *in his lap is Frank Northrup, the editor. Next to him is Sue Edwards. Back row is W. W. Davis, Charley Becker, publisher, and his son C. M. Becker. The latter and Sue Edwards must be typesetters as they are holding "sticks" full of hand-set type.*
Courtesy of the H. E. Ricker family

69

Harry Brown Bullen was twenty-four in 1889 when he established Stillwater's first lumber and coal yard. It started on South Main Street and then moved to the southeast corner of Husband and Eighth. He did a land office business. People used wood and coal for heat and some installed central heating with coal furnaces. Gas heating became available in 1918 or 1919. To protect their claims, settlers had to quickly build improvements on their lots, and they stood in line for lumber. Bullen was a member of the original townsite company and active in establishing Stillwater schools.
Courtesy of Harry B. Bullen, grandson

The earliest picture of Main Street, taken seven months after the drawing for business lots in June 1889 and nine months after the land run, is probably from Eighth and Main streets. Within two months, more than fifty frame business buildings had been completed.
Courtesy of the Oklahoma State University Library, Special Collections

Stillwater, Oklahoma, Jan. 11, 1890--Seven months old

A large "Welcome" banner stretched halfway across Main Street and citizens swarmed into town at Stillwater's first birthday celebration on April 22, 1890. The flag at left is above Amon Swope's Bank of Stillwater at the northwest corner of Ninth and Main streets. The Stillwater of today could look as primitive as this to its citizens of 2089, another century from now.
Photo courtesy of the Sheerar Museum, the John H. Barnes family

The Pacific Hotel in the nine hundred block of South Main Street was headquarters for teamsters who came to Stillwater during the heavy construction starting in 1889. The building just left of it is believed to be the third location of the Stillwater post office after it moved from the Swiler Bros. Store. Courtesy of the C. K. Bullen family

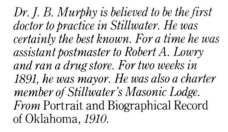

Dr. J. B. Murphy is believed to be the first doctor to practice in Stillwater. He was certainly the best known. For a time he was assistant postmaster to Robert A. Lowry and ran a drug store. For two weeks in 1891, he was mayor. He was also a charter member of Stillwater's Masonic Lodge. From Portrait and Biographical Record of Oklahoma, 1910.

Simon Peter Duck, patriarch of the Duck family, and his wife, Sarah Jane, homesteaded a quarter section of land that seemed far out in the country in 1889, but which is now a part of Stillwater. A native of Ohio, Duck was a Civil War veteran who fought at both Pea Ridge and Vicksburg. The Ducks were parents of seven sons and two daughters. The family was prominent in city history and Duck Street was named for them. S. P. Duck's homestead extended from present day Sixth Street north to Farm Road, and from Orchard Lane west to Western.
Courtesy of John E. Duck

A Stillwater business directory compiled less than a year after the land run lists two stage lines, two blacksmith shops, several sawmills, and most prominent pioneers. It was too early for phone numbers. Ninth Street was the dividing line for North and South Main.
Courtesy of the Clarence Bassler Heritage Collection, Stillwater Public Library

Main Street Grows With Stores and Banks

Since the time Charles and Sarah Donart homesteaded the quarter section at Perkins Road and Twelfth Street in 1889, the Donart clan has had great impact on many facets of Stillwater life, especially in teaching, public service, and banking. The original homestead is now Couch Park, and the Southside Baptist Church is on the site of the former Donart home. In this photo, taken in 1915, are: (children on front row) James Melvin, Louise, Roma, Helen, and Hazel Donart, Catherine Coffey, Wilberta Donart, and Lucius Coffey; (second row, seated) Mrs. Edward (Eda Donart) Millard, Charles and Sarah Donart, Louella Coffey, Rolland Millard, Earnest Coffee, Wilberta, Chauncey, Julia, and Harry Donart; (back row, standing) Clarence and Martha Donart, Edward Millard, Jennie Jones Donart, Herbert and Charles F. Donart, Cora Donart Coffey, Alma Cole Donart, Gladys, Carrie, and Julia Donart, and May Kinyon Donart.
Courtesy of Barbara Hartley Dunn, granddaughter of Charles Donart, and Mrs. C. E. (Ruth) Donart

Sam Miller's department store was the first in Stillwater. He started in the eight hundred block of Main two doors north of the New York Racket store. He later moved to the seven hundred block of Main and for a time he and Jake Katz were lively competitors.
Courtesy of Brenda Gould

Orlando M. Eyler opened the second grocery store in Stillwater in the nine hundred block of South Main. He was on the school board when the Stillwater system was organized and became mayor of Stillwater in 1895. He was an early leader in the Methodist Church. He spoke German well and people of German descent came from miles around to trade with him. He is pictured here with his family, (front row) W. C. (Bill), Orlando, Mrs. Eyler, and Frank; (back row) Dora (later Mrs. H. E. Ricker), Clara Louisa, and Fred. The latter became a butcher in the Eyler store. Courtesy of the H. E. Ricker family

Dominating the eight hundred block of Eighth and Main on the east side was the Stillwater National Bank, built in 1894. The Payne County Journal said "the bank was on the best corner in town and was built of native red and white sandstone, ornamented and designed in a most beautiful manner above which is inscribed in bright, golden letters, Stillwater State Bank." (The bank was first known as a state bank.) Shelly W. Keiser, who came from Illinois, was its principal founder. In 1909, Keiser sold his interests to the Berry family, who controlled the bank for years. Courtesy of the Oklahoma State University Library, Special Collections

A large awning extended across the front and part of the south side of the Youst Hotel for the first few years after its construction in 1894. Such awnings provided travelers with a sheltered place to sit and visit during evening hours.
Courtesy of Emma Ingersol Price

The Youst Hotel was an impressive sight on the northeast corner of Main and Eighth streets. This view also shows Stillwater's first street lighting system.
Courtesy of the Oklahoma State University Library, Special Collections

One of the earliest views of the O. M. Eyler grocery and the post office next to it are in this view from the southwest corner of Tenth and Main streets taken in 1892 or 1893. The first Stillwater post office was established shortly after the 1889 land run in a sixteen-by-twenty foot frame building at the corner of Thirteenth Street and Perkins Road in the store of Will and Ambrose Swiler. In June 1889, the Swilers moved to 908 South Main and took the post office with them. It remained there a short time, then moved several doors south. It next moved across the street next to O. M. Eyler where it remained for about ten years before moving to the northeast corner of Seventh and Main.
Courtesy of the Sheerar Museum and the C. K. Bullen family

For more than half a century, Jacob (Jake) Katz was considered the patriarch of the Stillwater business district. Born near Frankfurt, Germany, on September 13, 1873, Katz came to the United States in 1887 and then to Stillwater in 1894, when the above picture was taken. For a time he was apprentice to his uncle, Eli Youngheim, but in 1896 he started his own store in the eight hundred block of South Main Street. He was joined soon by his brother, Isaac (Ike), and their store became Katz Bros. The two later opened a store in Pawnee, and Ike chose to go there. Jake moved to the west side of Main in the seven hundred block and his store became the Boston Store. He remained there until 1913 when he moved to the east side of Main.
Courtesy of Helen Katz Goldman

76

When William A. Frick brought his family from Pennsylvania in 1896, he chose the southeast corner of Tenth and Main streets for his feed, seed, and hay store. The intersection was then in the heart of the business district. Both the buildings were a part of his operation, which he continued until the early 1920s. In this 1906 picture, Frick is seated on the wagon. On the porch of his store are his son Edward, his daughters Peggy and Violet, and his wife Kathleen. Violet, at this writing, lived east of Stillwater. The Lee Company now occupies this location.
Courtesy of Margaret Elledge

Santa Claus came to Stillwater in 1898, at least to the home of Harry and Narcissus May Donart at 401 South Duncan Street. The three Donart daughters, Ruth, far left, Julia, in the high chair, and Gladys, being embraced by Santa, seemed bewildered as they gazed upon gifts that included dolls, doll buggies, and a small organ. Santa was really their father, one of Stillwater's first school teachers, an early court clerk, and later bank cashier. The home was still standing in 1988, although greatly modified.
Courtesy of the
Richard F. Weilmuenster family

The first ten years of Stillwater are reflected in this picture of the eight hundred block of South Main Street, taken in 1899. On the left end of the block is Amon W. Swope's two-story frame building where he and T. W. Myton started the first bank and organized the Methodist Church. The first school was on the second floor. Next door is the jewelry store of the Grady brothers, Irby and Walter K., followed by Sam Miller's store, the first department store. In the background is Alcott School, completed at Duck and Eighth in 1896. The small white building to the left and on this side of Alcott is the earliest Baptist church. Opposite it, facing Eighth on the right, is the Methodist's first church.
Courtesy of the Oklahoma State University Library, Special Collections

The Railroad Arrives on Sunday Morning

Only the Cherokee Strip run of 1893 caused more excitement in Stillwater than the arrival of the railroad in 1900. As the Eastern

Oklahoma Railway completed laying the track into Stillwater, the construction train, pictured here, sounded its whistle at 9:00 A.M., Sunday, March 25. Churches stayed empty that morning as townspeople rushed to see the railroad. The Stillwater

Gazette estimated that seven hundred people turned out for the occasion. The track came from Ripley, across the Cimarron River and Boomer Creek to Stillwater and then to Pawnee.
Courtesy of Lawrence Gibbs

Even as tracks were laid into Stillwater, a depot was being built. The first was a wooden structure, which was replaced by the above depot in 1911. Before train service began, travelers depended on horse-drawn hacks for limousine service. Louis Snyder took passengers over hill and dale on the five-hour trip to Orlando, and W. W. Snyder hauled them to Wharton (Perry) in three-and-a-half hours to catch north and south bound trains.
Courtesy of the Oklahoma State University Library, Special Collections

Stillwater's first telephone service began in August 1899 when the Arkansas Telephone Company began operations at 814½ South Main over Fred Stallard's Saloon. Residence phones were one dollar a month. The operation became really professional when it moved to 724 South Main in 1901 and became known as Pioneer Telephone and Telegraph Company. Standing on the right, Paul Boone, who became manager in 1900, looks over the exciting new equipment. The company moved again in 1911 to 702 South Main and then in 1931 to 502 South Main.
Courtesy of Clarence Cowan

G. B. Waters' OK Store was in the middle of the seven hundred block of South Main Street, The driver of the wagon is Peter D. Curtis. Standing is John Kerby. Both homesteaded land south of Stillwater. The two used this wagon to move the O. K. Hotel at Ingalls at Stillwater about 1902. Courtesy of Mrs. Jim (Ruth) Wells

The First National Bank was started in 1899 from a consolidation of the Payne County Bank and the Farmers and Merchants Bank. The First National was first located near the center of the eight hundred block of South Main Street but in the summer of 1900 this new building was completed on the southwest corner of Eighth and Main. It has had two new buildings since then. On the second floor is the office of Dr. E. L. Moore, an early dentist. Courtesy of Mrs. Fay Hull

After a major fire in 1893 in the nine hundred block of South Main, M. W. J. Holt, a jeweler, pleaded with the town board to buy firefighting equipment. The board purchased an old barn and moved it to the northwest corner of Ninth and Lewis. This became the fire station. In 1900 this two-story station was erected there and it became fire department headquarters until 1974 when a new station was built at 1506 South Main. Holt became Stillwater's first fire chief in 1900.
Courtesy of the Stillwater Fire Department

Stillwater's first fire wagons were horse drawn, although at first, the fire department had to borrow horses from the Myers' Livery across the street. This wagon was retained for years and often appeared in parades.
Courtesy of the Sheerar Museum

Harry B. Bullen's fancy surrey was the envy of the town just before the turn of the century. Out for a spin are Bullen, his wife Carrie, his young son Clarence, and Miss Florence Felt. Clarence became mayor in 1924.
Courtesy of the C. K. Bullen family

From the time it was a village of three hundred, Stillwater had a community band that played concerts on Main Street. This one, probably in the 1890s, had some familiar names on its roster. Pictured are (front row left to right) Clarence Donart, Arthur B. McReynolds, Dr. J. B. Murphy,

L. O. Woods, John H. Barnes, Wilson Hand, Loyd Woods, and M. Talbot; (second row) Henry Hand, M. W. J. Holt (jeweler and first fire chief), Bill Amos, Dick Highmore, unidentified, Ed Means, and George Talbot; (third row) Arthur Adams (one of OAMC's first graduates), Ollie

Stevenson, unidentified, Ervin Lewis, Harry Donart (one of Stillwater's first teachers), unidentified, and Billy Zahl.
Courtesy of Barbara Hartley Dunn and Mrs. C. E. (Ruth) Donart

Stillwater's population was less than five hundred in 1900 when Louis J. Jardot and James W. Blouin joined in building the elegant Opera House at 116 East Ninth Street. Jardot manufactured the brick and did the construction. Blouin provided the financing and operated a furniture store on the ground floor. A patriotic observance was in progress when this view of the Opera House, with water tower in background, was taken in 1909.
Courtesy of the H. E. Ricker family

Dorcas Blouin, age two months, may be eyeing the construction of Stillwater's Opera House in this 1899 picture. Her father, James W. Blouin, helped finance the building. Dorcas' carriage matched the elegance of the Opera House. She grew up to be a Payne County deputy court clerk.
Courtesy of Marjalie Ransom Inciardi

William Jennings Bryan once made an eloquent speech from the stage of the Stillwater Opera House and Carry Nation brought her anti-saloon campaign to town. During her Opera House appearance, Carry sold small hatchets for fifty cents each to raise campaign money. The first talking pictures in Stillwater were shown at the Opera, which later became known as the Hollywood Theatre. Hypnotists, vaudeville acts, and slide lectures were booked regularly. The theatre was on the second floor.
Courtesy of Mr. and Mrs. Harold T. Jardot

Yost Lake was built in 1801 by the Santa Fe Railroad to serve as a watering station shortly after the first trains arrived in Stillwater. Two years later, Robert A.

Lowry organized a country club that obtained a lease on the property.
Courtesy of the NewsPress
Pierce Collection

The first pavilion at Yost Lake was usually crowded, as in this 1914 photo. Even into the post-World War II era, Yost Lake was Stillwater's favorite site for picnics and swimming, and owning a cabin there was a

status symbol. It is still an attractive resort but nearby lakes and state parks have made it much less exclusive.
Courtesy of Forrest K. Boaz

Yost had a train stop in the early days and less affluent citizens without cars spent a dime for a one-way trip. Two ladies are awaiting the train back to Stillwater.
Courtesy of Forrest K. Boaz

When a photographer snapped a picture of mail carrier Shurrell Houston, he also captured a rare view of South Main and Seventh streets. On the southeast corner was the Stillwater Dry Goods Company on the site now occupied by Katz department store and on the northeast corner was the building that became the post office in about 1906 and later the M. G. Searcy Grocery. The wagon at right was filled with wagon wheels, including one hanging from the rear like a spare tire. The scene was probably in 1902 or 1903.
Courtesy of Sheerar Museum

Stillwater people needed no alarm clocks the first few years. Donkeys started braying as early as five A.M. in livery stables all around Main Street. Here, Albert W. Ahrberg posed in front of his livery barn next door to the historic Commercial Hotel that operated at Ninth and Husband streets for forty years. The Caywood family first owned the hotel, possibly as early as 1900. In 1925, Mr. and Mrs. T. F. McWherter leased it and operated it the next fifteen years. The hotel was replaced in the early 1940s by Upton Ward's Buick Agency. Courtesy of Jean White Stanbery

Stillwater became an ice manufacturing center in 1900 when Frank Lahman opened the first ice plant on East Sixth Street near the railroad tracks. He also manufactured ice wagons and expanded with plants in Blackwell, Ponca City, and Pawnee. Near the two-horse wagon above are Bill Powell and Orville Blossom. Red Tole is near the second wagon. Walter Rossander is by the truck near the metal shed. By the truck in right foregound are John Gardner and D. Bradford Manning. The city used the large tank in the back-ground to store bunker fuel, a low grade of oil for back-up power in case the city was plunged into darkness. Courtesy of D. Bradford Manning

After the land runs of 1889 and 1893, and the fights for the townsite and the county seat, Fred Knowles felt it was time for a pause that refreshes. He obtained the first Coca-Cola franchise in Stillwater and is shown here making the rounds.
Courtesy of Forrest K. Boaz

This view is looking north on the west side of Main from Eighth Street in about 1913. On the corner is the State Bank of Commerce. In the basement was Stillwater's only public bathhouse and a barber shop. The outside stairway forked at the second floor. Upstairs left was the Pioneer Tele-phone Company. To the right were a room where men played pitch and gambled, and the office of early dentist R. A. Barron. Frank J. Wikoff was bank president and C. E. Steen, cashier.
Courtesy of the Oklahoma State University Library, Special Collections

Stillwater had one asset in the early 1900s that it does not have today: a rapid transit system. At least that's what this vehicle was called. It meandered from town to campus and to the railroad station.
Courtesy of Forrest K. Boaz

Charles Duck (left) and brother Will spent much time taking care of farming chores on the family homestead, but they also operated one of Stillwater's best blacksmith shops, housed in a fancy brick building. It was located in the one hundred block of East Seventh, facing south. The wagon in front has a place in history, too. It's one of the first Watkins Products delivery vans.
Courtesy of John E. Duck

John and Mary Cole settled on a farm northwest of Stillwater in 1900 near the present-day corner of Washington and Hall of Fame and the site of the Farmhouse Fraternity. Young men of the town came to court their attractive daughter, Lula, pictured here. This one, known only as "Mr. Evans," apparently had the inside track because of this fancy set of wheels.
Courtesy of Barbara Hartley Dunn
and Mrs. C. E. (Ruth) Donart

Charles Ingersol peers from his rural mail delivery wagon in 1907. His Route 5 took him across Stillwater Creek to Mehan and then north near Spring Valley School. Ingersol began postal work in 1905 or 1906. He sorted his mail before starting and put letters in envelope slots along the walls of the wagon. He carried a pouch to sell stamps along the way.
Courtesy of Emma Ingersol Price

When the Drumright oil field opened, George Knowles expanded by opening markets in Cushing and Drumright. An onlooker watches as he travels in style. His 1912 auto was the first Cadillac in Stillwater.
Courtesy of Forrest K. Boaz

George Franklin Knowles and his wife, Maude, made the Land Run of 1889 and opened a meat market on Stillwater's Main Street. Barely visible through the window are meat cuts hanging from the ceiling. Hitching posts and a rail provide parking in front.
Courtesy of Forrest K. Boaz

The New York Racket store has succeeded Amon Swope's bank and the Tornado Store at the corner of Ninth and Main streets in this photo taken around 1910. Grady Bros., jewlers, and Sam Miller's department store are still adjacent. The two-story white frame building in the background is the second courthouse. Brenda Gould, whose father, Parley, worked in the Racket store, described it as "a typical old time general merchandising store that carried almost everything but groceries."
Courtesy of the Sheerar Museum,
"The Story of Stillwater, Oklahoma, The World's Safest City,"
Junior Chamber of Commerce, 1954

As motion pictures became popular, a new theatre, the Camera, made its appearance in about 1916 just north of the Youst Hotel. The poster in front on the left announces that The Other Man, *starring Fatty Arbuckle, will be the next attraction. In the silent movie era, a pianist played accom-* paniment to the film action. The star pianist at Stillwaer movie houses, including the Camera, Mecca, and Alamo, was Ruth Donart.
Courtesy of the NewsPress,
Pierce Collection

Chapter
7

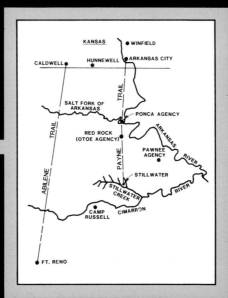

THE COUNTY SEAT FIGHT

After the drawing for townsite lots, Orlando M. Eyler wasted no time opening a grocery store in a choice location in the nine hundred block of South Main. In an ad in the small village's first newspaper, the *Oklahoma Standard*, he included a verse that typified the spirit of Stillwater's pioneers.

> So now I take this time to say
> I'm in Stillwater here to stay,
> I give the flies no chance to blow,
> The moss to sprout or grass to grow.

Certainly the leaders in the small village let no grass grow under their feet. Even while the townsite fight was underway, they began another struggle—this time to make Stillwater the county seat. Although the population was only just over three hundred and the town made up of a few dirt streets, they recognized the importance of the county seat designation to the future of Stillwater. So confident were they that on June 11, 1889, they reserved a lot for a new courthourse. Then they went to work with vigor.

The county seat fight was for a time even more bitter than the townsite fuss and almost resulted in violence and gunplay. A dozen or so small communities had sprung up in the area and each dreamed of being chosen as the seat. The two major contenders other than Stillwater were Payne Center and Perkins.

Payne Center was a small village about three miles south of Stillwater just off present day South Husband Street. Its organizer and spokesman was Patrick H. Guthrey, a devoted follower of David L. Payne. Some settlers said Payne himself had once surveyed the land for a townsite when he thought his Boomers might remain in Oklahoma.

Guthrey was determined to honor Payne. He called the settlement Payne Center and then sought to have the county called Payne with Payne Center as the seat. He and his followers set aside forty acres for a townsite. This would extend westward from Husband Street. On the extreme west edge he established a cemetery. An additional tract was set aside on the east for the anticipated growth of the town. This extended all the way to present Highway 177. A small school called Payne Center was erected on the eastern edge of the land.

The Payne Center settlers erected a one-story octagon-shaped building that served as courthouse, city hall, and home of its mayor, Patrick Guthrey. South of this building was a town well, post office, blacksmith shop, and grocery store. Guthrey was joined soon by his son, Early Bee Guthrey, who had just finished law school at the University of Michigan. Young Guthrey was also a printer, and he took over a Payne Center newspaper, the *Oklahoma Hawk*.

As the county seat contest began, Payne Center's leaders prepared a map of the site showing the location of a future courthouse and university. It showed names and locations of planned streets and other improvements. The population was 142 as Payne Center filed application with the Guthrie Land Office to be county seat.

Meantime, Stillwater was taking a different approach to win the county seat. Its leaders prepared a special presentation and quietly sent one of its most persuasive young attorneys, Frank A. Hutto, to Washington. His assignment was to persuade Congress to add several small townships in the Cherokee Outlet to the county. This would make Stillwater the geographical center. Then he was to present Stillwater as the ideal county seat.

If there were any doubts about the issue, this strategy may have turned the tide. Hutto did a masterful job. He persuaded Congress to add Eden, Rose, Glencoe, Walnut, and Rock townships to the county, although the latter two were transferred to Noble County after the Cherokee Outlet was opened to settlement in 1893. His visit changed the shape of Payne County. He also made a strong impression on the Kansas delegation as he told of Stillwater's advantages as a county seat. When he returned, the issue was for all practical purposes settled.

Unaware of this, Payne Center and Perkins supporters became impatient. Their actions almost resulted in violence and gunplay. As historian Dr. B. B. Chapman recorded:

> One summer evening in 1889 a group of 30 or 40 men from Payne Center proposed to move to that place such county records as were at Stillwater. About dusk they reached Stillwater Creek, just below its junction with Boomer creek, where they were met by twice their number of men from Stillwater. Some men on both sides of the creek were armed. Robert A. Lowry was the spokesman for the Stillwater men. He talked with the Payne Center group, across the creek, and they agreed to abandon their scheme.

A few days later a group of Perkins men gathered on the banks of Stillwater Creek and argued bitterly with a Stillwater contingent over who should have rights to keep county records until a seat was chosen. As the number of Stillwater defenders kept growing, the Perkins group decided not to force the issue.

After the confrontations, Patrick Guthrey began to have second thoughts about the whole matter. He sensed the tide was turning to Stillwater. And perhaps it seems a bit shocking, but he began to believe this might be a good thing. It was the location of Stillwater Creek that largely influenced his thinking. Payne Center had no water supply other than a few wells. Stillwater Creek would always provide a basic supply for Stillwater. Guthrey concluded that Stillwater, not Payne Center, would be the town of the future he had envisioned. He asked to meet with a group of Stillwater leaders to work out a compromise on the county seat issue.

Stillwater responded quickly and appointed a committee consisting of Amon W. Swope, a banker; John R. Clark, a real estate man; and Robert Lowry. Guthrey offered to cease all Payne Center efforts for the county seat and to give full support to Stillwater's claim if the county were named for the former leader he idolized, David L. Payne. Stillwater's committee was elated. The sentiment was already almost unanimous for naming the county Payne and some were already calling it that. They agreed and happily shook hands. On May 2, 1890, Congress officially designated seven counties in Oklahoma, the sixth of which was to be called Payne, with Stillwater as the county seat.

This should have provided a happy ending to the story, but an anticlimactic fight was still to be fought. Having cast his lot with Stillwater, Patrick Guthrey decided there was no reason for Payne Center to exist further. His son, Early Bee, moved the *Oklahoma Hawk* to Stillwater. Guthrey then built a fence around five acres of Payne Center that included the business area. He refused to let people enter, even to pick up mail, and guarded the site with a shotgun. Some Payne Center settlers were already angry with Guthrey for his compromise on the county seat. Now they were furious. After a few days, Guthrey relented and opened the gates, but the die was cast. The community began a decline. The small cemtery was taken over for farming. Its crosses and headstones were pulled up or plowed under and the names of those buried there faded into oblivion as did Payne Center itself. The small community's post office closed on February 12, 1894.

Few men had more impact on laying the foundation for Stillwater than Amon W. Swope. A native of Pennsylvania, and later a Winfield, Kansas, banker, he arrived in Stillwater in June 1889 at age forty-six. In the first two-story building on the northwest corner of Ninth and Main he established the first bank, the Bank of Stillwater, later called the Citizens Bank. He organized the Methodist Church, which met in his building. In 1890, he was named mayor of the struggling village. When Perkins challenged Stillwater for the county seat, he was chairman of a committee to represent Stillwater.
From Portrait and Biographical Record of Oklahoma, *1910*

Galvanized metal wash tubs, buckets, and kerosene lanterns hung from the wall of O. M. Eyler's grocery store in this interior photo, probably taken in 1895. The black boxes in center were filled with crackers. When the store opened in 1889, it was lighted by kerosene lamps but these have been replaced by an electric light suspended from the ceiling. His son, Fred, left foreground, was a butcher. Eyler is on the right. Courtesy of the H. E. Ricker family

Payne Center, Stillwater's rival for the county seat, was three miles south of town in 1889. This would now be between Forty-fourth and Fiftieth Avenue. The Payne Center School was at the intersection of Fifty-sixth and Highway 177. The small community boasted a city hall-courthouse (which was also the mayor's home), a post office, newspaper, and cemetery. Legends say David L. Payne had chosen the site for his future home.
Map by Mike Shores, courtesy of the Community Development Department, City of Stillwater

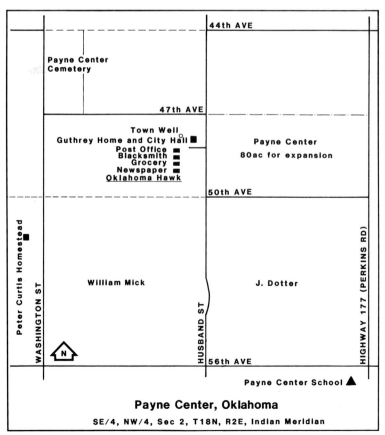

Oklahoma Hawk.

VOLUME 2.   STILLWATER, PAYNE CO., OKLAHOMA, THURSDAY, SEPT. 3, 1891.   NUMBER

SCRAPS

Gov. Steele is gone again.

The Kickapoos are ready to treat after so long a time.

All the beer saloons in the Chickasaw country have been closed.

In Terrill's poem he expresses himself in favor of free whiskey.

New York suffered great loss of life and property last week by fire.

Gen. Alger says Blaine will be the republican candidate for president.

The governor is gone but he will be back when the rush comes. Wonder if he wants a claim.

India wants to be an independent government. Great Britian may look out for another revolution.

One of the members of the Interstate Commerce Commission has died and a great influence will be brought to bear upon the president to appoint a Trans-Mississippi man.

The Guthrie Capital and Ok. City Gazette are "scrapping" as it were over which shall have Mrs. Rock's Press. It the Judge has no objection we suggest that she give them both a Press and stop the little rack et.

A Kansas man is known as a "Jayhawker" and for every state we have some peculiar name. When Oklahoma becomes a state some man like Vic Murdock whose head is ever full of the eternal fitness of things will "dub" us the "Sooners."

The county attorney of Saline county, Kan., is known as "old necessity" because "Necessity knows no law." There are many old necessities in Oklahoma.—Yukon Courier.

If that is the way you size them up we've got an "old Necessity" in this county. He exercises "Judicial Power" however, instead of being county attorney.

—Ramy & Collins are painting the front of their 9th. Ave. saloon.

—Mr. and Mrs. Sidney Phillippe

Died.

MURPHY.—August 29th, 1891, at McPherson Kansas, Nelly Bly Murphy, aged 11 months and 6 days.

The deceased was the infant child of Dr. and Mrs. Murphy, of this city. It had been sick for several days and the doctors thought a change of climate would improve and help it this advice the doctor left last Thursday for Kansas with the child but it was beyond human power to save and the little one died at McPherson a few days after their departure and was returned to this city last Monday. The doctor and family have the sincere sympathy of a large circle of friends.

A rosebud from Heaven
To sweet for this life,
'Twas called to its home again
Away from all strife.

Its petals unfolded
Just enough for us to see
How beautiful in maturity
The blossom would be.

But the Angels it seems wanted
Dear little Nelly Bly
So they've called her to live,
In that sweet bye and bye,

She will wait over the river
With a baby Angels drum
And beat time for us
When our call shall come.

Let us bless the little Angel
And rejoice that she's free
From the sins of the world
That tempt you and me.

Let us hope in eternity
We'll meet her so fair
In the home that's prepared
For the good over there.

Not Successfully Refuted.

From the Plaindealer.

The HAWK last week bursted

WEDDING BELLS.

ADAMS-KINYON.

At the residence of Mr. E. P. Downs, 2½ miles north of Stillwater, on Wednesday, Aug. 26, at 1 p. m. Miss Allie Kinyon and Mr. Walter Adams were united in marriage by Rev. Webster Full, according to the ritual of the M. E. Church, south. After the ceremony and congratulations a beautiful dinner was served, and all did full justice to the eatables while jests and laughter enlivened all. Several useful presents were received by the young couple, as mementos of the happy occasion.

We notice that the bride was charming in a costume of Princess of Wales blue Ottoman silk with braid trimmings and lace. The groom wearing the conventional black.

"Happy is the bride the sun shines on," they say and we trust life will always be as bright for them as was their wedding day. Those present were the families of Mr. W. H. H. Adams, Mr. Downs, J. K. Carr and daughters Misses Dora and Carrie, Misses Pearl and Hattie Jenkins, Master Noah Morris, of Augusta, Kan., Rev. and Mrs. W. Full, Mrs. John Bryson and daughter Alma, Mr. and Mrs. E. R. Lane and baby Bertha. Just before we left for home in the evening all went to the grove near by where Mr. Lane made two negatives of the group which by some freak of fortune were both remarkably good, and the pictures will form a pleasant reminder of "auld lang syne" many years hence. A very pleasant affair dinner was given at Mr. Adams, Sr. next day.

We'll wish for them the best of life, May sorrow pass them by, And if they chance to need a friend May friends be ever nigh.

We know that they are happy now, For life is in its prime, But fairest things o. earth will fade Beneath the touch of time.

May they be like clouds of summer,
Silver lined on every side.
And when life's sun is sinking,
In the golden, western skies,
May the light of Heaven shine brighter,
In your dim and faded eyes.

And when you pass from earth away
May angels from the Strand,
Bear your souls from earth below
Up to that glorious land,
That in the City of Delight,
Where Christ your Lord is King.

And why the angels sing.
Sing praise to Him who gave you life
And comfort on your way,
From Earth below, to Heaven above,
Through out eternity.

The company was then ushered into a repast, the equal of which is seldom seen.

The groom Mr. McClain is one of Payne Counties nicest young men. He is a school teacher and has a claim four and a half miles west of Stillwater where they will reside. The bride is loved by all who know her, and has made an impression on us as few young ladies ever did. She is the daughter of R. D. Bowers who is one of Payne county's most energetic farmers.
A. GUEST.

—Will the ever come when the old soldiers who draw pensions will be released from the claim which the republican party now assumes to hold over them? The republican editors of this territory and also of Kansas and other places talk as though a pension had no right to vote anything but the republican ticket. If the great army of pensioners are not freemen from principle, we certainly ought as fealt to land with them that if it comes to the trouble with them the Gazette is

The Governor.

From the Capital.

Governor Steele left on the 5 o'clock train this morning for Washington to advise the president and the department about the new country which is on the eve of opening. He told a State Capital reporter yesterday that he had recently written the secretary of the interior whether the opening would likely be by September 9th, as he would make his arrangements to be back by that time in case it should occur by that time. The telegram he received yesterday granting him fifteen days leave of absence also stated and don't think it will open until after the time you mention." The governor thought it would not be before the 12th, and perhaps not until the 20th of September. He will return by the 15th and sooner if he can get his work disposed of in time. At all events he will be here on the great day.

New Evidence.

Capital.

The Sac and Fox and Pottawattomie countries are said to be filled with persons who have gone in to select the best lands, says the O. C. Gazette. The enterprising photographer with kodak is there collecting evidence which will be sold to the highest bidder in future contests before the land office.

Charlie Willis and family have gone to Kansas to put up fruit for the winter.

Deputy Marshal Taylor was in Guthrie last Monday and returned to this city Monday night.

Supt. Foster and J. E. Sater were at Perkins Tuesday looking over the new bridge.

Allan Christie has returned to Winfield where he expects to enter school on the 14th, of this month.

Quite a crowd of Stillwater people were at Perkins last Tuesday attending the bridge celebration.

Early B. (Bee) Guthrey used his Payne Center newspaper, the Oklahoma Hawk, *as a propaganda medium during the county seat fight. Guthrey's press was homemade from an old grave marker. He handset the type and then inked pages with a hand roller. After the county seat issue was settled, he moved the* Hawk *to Stillwater. In this issue (first column) he worries that, since Kansas people are being called "Jayhawkers," someone may get the idea to call Oklahoma people "Sooners."*
Courtesy of the Richard F. Weilmuenster family

Dan W. Murphy, founder of the Stillwater Gazette *in December 1889, pays a visit to the building of another early newspaper, the* Oklahoma Hawk *in Payne Center. Murphy receives a friendly greeting from the deer that roamed the Stillwater Valley then, but the* Hawk *publisher, Early Bee Guthrey, was not on the scene.*
Courtesy of the Richard F. Weilmuenster family

Frank A. Hutto was only twenty-seven when he was sent on a secret mission to Washington to secure the county seat for Stillwater. His efforts were later rewarded as he became the first elected Payne County attorney. Hutto was also a scholar. In 1898 he was named chairman of a newly created department of history and political economy at OAMC and for a time was director of the college library.
Courtesy of
Mr. and Mrs. F. W. Weilmuenster

The most visible remnant today of Payne Center is this widely-traveled schoolhouse. In the early 1920s, it was transferred to the south edge of Stillwater and became Pleasant View School. In about 1960, it was moved to the rodeo grounds west of Perkins where it still stands, although somewhat modified. The Pleasant View pupils from the 1950s shown here include such familiar Stillwater names as Blankinship, Hiner, McGuire, Sykora, Tarpey, and Grooms. Teachers were Mrs. Pearl Spurr, far left and Bill Needham, far right.
Courtesy of Mary A. Blankinship

Payne County's first courthouse, completed in 1891, cost only four hundred dollars. Before it was built, court was held in the Presbyterian Church sanctuary. The courthouse was destroyed by fire on December 26, 1894 after sparks from wood stoves ignited rubbish on the floor. The most memorable trial here was that of Arkansas Tom Jones of the Doolin gang after the 1893 gunfight at Ingalls.
Courtesy of the NewsPress

Payne County's second courthouse was built in 1895. On the southwest corner of the lots were a tin building used for a jail, and a pen for several bloodhounds. The out-side stairway was equipped to serve as gallows, but no one was ever hanged there. Sixth from the right on the first row, standing, is Walter E. Going, county treasurer from 1921-1924.
Courtesy of
Mr. and Mrs. Lyle Winterhalter

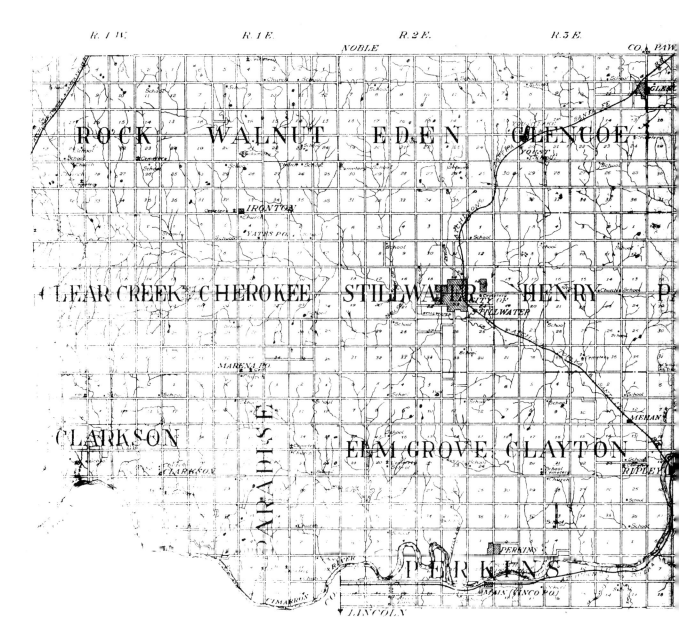

Payne County officers of 1906 gather on the steps of the frame courthouse: (left to right) George Dollinger, deputy county treasurer; Charles ("Elmer") Donart, deputy court clerk; Ralph Smith, register of deeds; Ed McCoy, sheriff; Henry Jerome, county treasurer; Sam Smith, county judge; Perry Hays, deputy register of deeds; Maye Potter, abstractor; Orlow Lowry, court stenographer; and the courthouse mascot, Pep, the dog on the right, and his friend on the left, behind Ralph Smith.
Courtesy of Barbara Hartley Dunn and Mrs. C. E. (Ruth) Donart

The shape of Payne County across the northern border was once considerably different, as shown in this 1907 map. Originally, Congress added Rock, Walnut, Eden, Glencoe, and Rose townships to the county to make Stillwater almost in the geographical center and a logical county seat. When the counties were reshaped by the Oklahoma Constitutional Convention of 1907, Rock and Walnut townships were transferred back to Noble County.
From the Payne County Almanac, 1907, courtesy of Elton Nixon

Robert A. Lowry, left, and County Commissioner Chris Holzer, next to him, were present on January 17, 1918, for laying of the new courthouse cornerstone. Citizens that day placed in the stone a box containing a history of Stillwater, a picture of the previous courthouse, and other historical documents, and Lowry said, "Except earthquake, cyclone or bombardment,....the papers entombed today will not be viewed again for hundreds of years."
Courtesy of Chris S. Holzer and the NewsPress

101

The court clerk's office in 1905 boasted an
electric fan for cooling, a wood stove for
heating, and a spittoon and wash basin for
Court Clerk Harry Donart. Other county
officers were in rented rooms around town.
In 1916, a grand jury convened to investi-
gate the need for a new courthouse called
the building "ugly and unfit to be a courthouse" and the jail "unfit to be called a jail
and should be called a kennel unfit for
human habitation." The jury recom-
mended a new courthouse to go on "the
beautiful shady grove site."
Courtesy of Barbara Hartley Dunn
and Mrs. C. E. (Ruth) Donart

A sign urging citizens to buy war savings stamps is in the foreground of a new Payne County courthouse under construction in May 1918. Excavation for the building started in October 1917, the cornerstone was laid January 26, 1918, and a house warming was held as the courthouse officially opened January 25, 1919. A $100,000 bond issue was passed in 1916, but the final cost of the project was $153,000.
Courtesy of the NewsPress,
Pierce Collection

Payne County's courthouse underwent major remodeling after a $995,000 bond issue passed in 1966. The county chose to make an addition extending the west side rather than build an entirely new building.
Photo by the author

Chapter 8

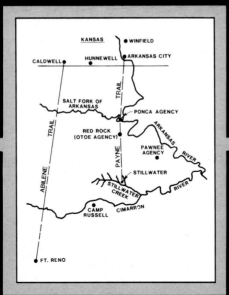

THE EARLY SCHOOLS AND CHURCHES

Lessons in reading, writing, and arithmetic for children of Stillwater's pioneers began unofficially near Stillwater Creek shortly after the run of April 22, 1889. Parents were concerned because many had held their children out of school for a term while they awaited the land run. G. E. Fuss settled his family near the site of Couch's 1884 Boomer encampment, living in a dugout while he built a one-room log cabin. When he finished the cabin in late May, it became a "subscription" school room. Parents in the area paid a fee so their children could attend and make up for lost time.

From the beginning, the founding fathers gave education a high priority. The city charter adopted August 19, 1889 provided for a board of education of three members, empowered the city to levy taxes for schools, to purchase school sites, and to erect buildings. The city set aside several lots for school buildings.

The first school board consisted of Parker Milligan, Charles F. Willis, and Nathan Davis. The board quickly hired its faculty—one teacher—to start teaching in September. Edward F. Clark not only was the first school teacher but the first to hold the title of principal in Stillwater schools.

On Monday morning, September 30, 1889, school opened officially in Stillwater for the first time as thirty youngsters of varying ages trudged down the dirt streets to the town's first two-story building on the northwest corner of Ninth and Main. Downstairs, Amon W. Swope would open the town's first bank. Upstairs was a large room, the only room in town suitable for meetings. The first Sunday School classes were held there as were other town meetings. The school board decided it was the only place in the village equipped for classes. Professor Clark, as he was called, taught all five grades.

While this was a beginning, it was still a subscription school, and the town leaders were anxious to get free public schools in operation. By mutual agreement between the town council and the school board, Hays Hamilton was appointed assessor. He promptly assigned values to Stillwater property and assessments were made to raise funds for schools. By December 1889, the school board had raised $185 for a budget and immediately inaugurated its free public school. By this time, enrollment had reached seventy-three.

In the summer of 1890, Stillwater set up a special three-month term to help children make up schooling missed during the early part of 1889. Edward F. Clark became ill and was replaced by Harry Donart. As enrollment continued to grow, the school board set up three school rooms. Donart completed Clark's term in the Swope building and then started classes in a cottonwood building at 119 West Ninth. It was then owned by Parker Milligan, a school board member. It is now a parking lot. John R. Holliday continued classes in the Swope building and Vincent Confrey was employed to teach at the northeast corner of Eighth and Main. Donart reported that sixty-six pupils were in the four grades he taught.

The new school system formally organized in 1891 and became School District 16. The school board then consisted of Orlando M. Eyler, Hays Hamilton, and Amon Swope. This board erected Stillwater's first school building, a two-room frame structure on the east side of Lewis street between Eleventh and Twelfth streets. In the fall of 1892, another building, almost a duplicate of the first, was built on Main Street between Second and Third streets where the school administration building now stands.

Life was hard for both teachers and pupils in Stillwater's first school rooms. For blackboards, carpenters nailed several boards together and painted them black. Desks and seats for the children were made from native cottonwood lumber. The seats were so high from the floor that some smaller children's feet did not reach the floor. The backs of the chairs were at right angles to the seats and very uncomfortable. Donart described the seats as "instruments of torture." He let his smaller pupils sit on the floor.

No textbooks were adopted in the first few years. Each child brought to school whatever books he used if he had attended school somewhere else. There were as many different textbooks as there were pupils. In Donart's memoirs, he described how he conducted classes:

I cut up old readers, pasting the simple words on cardboard, each word on a strip, these were piled at random in a box. Each child was handed a small pile of these strips, then I both wrote and printed a word on the board and they were to find that word in their strips, thus they were taught reading and spelling. A large number of sticks of different lengths from which we built rail fences and pig pens taught them numbers. For language and composition I assembled a variety of interesting pictures also pasted on cardboard, about which they constructed stories to be recited in class.

And in 1891, Rev. Simon P. Myers, president of the school board, reported after an inspection:

"...the room is small; the seats close together... the room is very uncomfortable in cold weather. The pupils next to the stove are too warm for comfort or health; those farther...suffer with cold....On windy days, the dust and dirt blows into the room so as to make it unpleasant. On such days, the noise caused by the wind makes it very difficult for teacher and pupils to understand one the other."

From these beginnings, Stillwater's school system began to grow. Principal Clark taught classes of highest ranking students in the North Methodist Church at Eighth and Duncan until 1891, when he became a faculty member at Oklahoma A&M College. The town council had in 1889 set aside lots on the northeast corner of West Ninth and Duck streets for schools. The Carey frame building opened there in 1893. The town bosted its first version of a high school when the Alcott School started on the same lots in 1896. This corner may be the most noted in school history as the new Horace Mann School replaced the Carey building in 1910, and in 1921 still another building, the new junior high, was erected on that site.

James Harrison (Harry) Donart taught in the subscription school started in 1889 on the second story of the Bourdett building at Ninth and Main. He would have fit well into the mainstream one hundred years later. He loved to exercise and jog and he was still practicing archery at age ninety-one. He was one of the village's best dressed men, as evidenced in this photo with the Independent Order of Odd Fellows emblem around his shoulders. Donart's pupils sat on hard wooden benches and his blackboard consisted of two boards painted black. Donart was later associated with the Stillwater National Bank for many years. Courtesy of the Richard F. Weilmuenster family

On September 30, 1889, school officially opened in Stillwater on the second floor of this frame two-story building at Ninth and Main Streets. The structure was briefly known as the Bourdett Building but is remembered historically as the Swope Building where Amon W. Swope and T. W. Myton operated Stillwater's first bank and a grocery store on the ground floor. The men in the foreground were intently observing the weighing of a bale of cotton, which legends say was the first bale brought to Stillwater.
Courtesy of the C. K. Bullen family

When the Stillwater school system was formally organized in 1891, the board erected the town's first school building on Lewis Street between Eleventh and Twelfth, facing west. In the fall of 1892, a similar two-room frame building, as shown, was erected on Main between Second and Third streets. The Rev. Simon P. Myers, Presbyterian church minister and president of the school board, described the buildings as cold and uncomfortable.
Courtesy of Mrs. Jim (Ruth) Wells

Some townspeople accused the school board of being extravagant in 1895 when it wanted to build Alcott School, but when completed in 1896 it was hailed as Stillwater's first high school. Alcott had six rooms but enrollment was small and the Masonic Lodge took over the second floor. The school was on Duck Street between Eighth and Ninth.
Courtesy of the
Richard F. Weilmuenster family

This is Stillwater high school's student body in 1901, just five years after the opening of Alcott. The town's population was about five hundred. Pictured are: (first row) Adrian Randall, C. B. Duck, Vernie Danner, Charles Thatcher, Finus McReynolds, Stewart Smith, Earl Kline, and Hugh Chamness; (second row) Blanche Sleen, Dollie Blancett, Clarence Dalton, Flossie Lewis, Nettie Cook, Lottie Austin, Fannie Hedges, Mable Bourdett, Martha Duck, Charles ("Elmer") Donart, Hester Thatcher, and Robert Bilyeu; (third row) Edna Stowe, Ray Blancett, Iva Hand, unidentified, Rosa Studebaker, unidentified, Clara Weirman, Eda Donart, Maude Chamness, Vida Meeks, Zella Hanner, and Alberta Maroney. Teachers are Jesse Thatcher, Josephine Gray, and R. H. Ewing.
Courtesy of Barbara Hartley Dunn and Mrs. C. E. (Ruth) Donart

By 1909, Stillwater felt the need for another school to accommodate the growing high school age group. After another fuss, the city voted to build Horace Mann School on lots adjoining Alcott School. It was opened in 1910. Elementary pupils continued at Alcott. Junior high and high school students moved to Horace Mann.
From Bronze and Blue, *1916*

For more than ten years, Alcott and Horace Mann schools stood side by side on Duck Street between Eighth and Ninth streets. In 1921, Horace Mann was demolished to make room for a new school that was at various times called high school, junior high, North High, and middle school. Alcott remained standing adjacent to the new school for several years.
Courtesy of the city of Stillwater

Pleasant Valley School, at Nineteenth Street and Sangre Road, was far out in the country when it opened as early as 1895. Its former students and Stillwater historians won a battle in 1987 to restore the school and to keep it at its original location. Behind the school was a woodshed where coal and corncobs were stored, and where pupils were paddled. Eight grades were taught in the one-room school, which opened each day with the Lord's Prayer. Pleasant Valley was a community center for church, pie suppers, and meetings. It closed shortly after World War II began, but its memories linger on.
Courtesy of the NewsPress

Little Pleasant Hill School on the road to McMurtry Lake opened its doors shortly after the Land Run of 1889. Its ruins are still there. Pioneer names such as Lile, Madison, Randolph, Laughlin, Williams, Fritchman, Schwartz, and Gates are associated with it.
Courtesy of Mrs. Margaret Mick

School records show that Lincoln School, with four classrooms at 215 East Twelfth, was under construction in 1898, but the earliest student or faculty records are for 1900. The building behind the school indicates Lincoln had outside facilities for a time. It was rebuilt in 1948 and an auditorium added. It is now a bus barn and food service building.
Courtesy of the
Richard F. Weilmuenster family

Jefferson School once stood between the three hundred and four hundred blocks of South Main. It was built in 1901, replacing a small frame building that served as one of the town's first two schools. Four grades were taught at Jefferson, which had two classrooms on the first floor and two on the second. The school bus was remodeled in 1910 and again in 1938. During still another remodeling in 1970, part of it was demolished, and the building was converted to the Board of Education building.
Courtesy of the
Richard F. Weilmuenster family

Old South High—Storehouse of Memories

Stillwater's greatest storehouse of memories is perhaps old South High at 1100 South Duncan. This is the way it appeared in its glory days. South High was built in 1919 and remained the high school until the early 1940s, after which it was converted to a junior high. It was Stillwater's first real high school, since it far exceeded little Alcott and Horace Mann. In the first years, Claud Baird taught shop in a small building north of the school and, in another area, Katie Kirkpatrick converted part of the yard into a garden to teach agriculture. The small basketball court was in the basement and the auditorium was on the second floor, west side. Hundreds of Stillwater residents attended the school.
Courtesy of Winfrey D.
and Barbara Houston

Hamilton Field was named for Ralph Hamilton, back row center, who coached Stillwater High School athletics from 1920 to 1958. With him is his 1931 basketball team: (front row) Lee Perry, Kenneth Gallagher, Clark Whitely (captain), and Charles Rice; (back row) Glenn Burnham, Hugh Hawley, Hamilton, Jack Burns, and Max Hanson. "If he were coaching today, he'd be fired," said Hanson. "He carried a barrel stave to football practice and whacked the running backs to make them move faster. He was tough but we all liked him."
Courtesy of Charles Rice

South High students in the 1930s gather around a favorite teacher, Faye McWethy, on the right at the south entrance. Facing camera is Norton Higgins, who became a senior executive of DuPont Company in Wilmington, Delaware. Girl in foreground is Teddy Price, daughter of Superintendent E. L. Price. Behind Higgins is football co-captain Robert Whitenton.
Courtesy of Bill Simank

Florence Severson, long-time English and journalism teacher at South High, shows off her new Studebaker in 1938. She is remembered for restarting the Bronze and Blue *yearbook after it had been discontinued for seventeen years.*
Courtesy of Bill Simank

When some students began missing class regularly, South High principal Walter McCollom suspected hookey playing. Like most principals, he knew what to do. He drove his Ford V-8 to the American Legion pool hall, rounded up the culprits, and brought them back to class. Left to right, in this 1939 group, were Turner P. (Junior) Hall, McCollom, Dick Reddington, and James (Pete) Weaver.
Courtesy of Bill Simank

South High's most famous graduate was Erskine Hill, Class of '38. In December 1977 he became a four-star general in the U.S. Air Force and in 1984 he was named to the Oklahoma Hall of Fame, but at South High he was known for his outstanding achievements in music. With the clarinet, he took first place, competing at Enid, Tonkawa, and Winfield, Kansas. He was named all-state band winner in 1935, 1936, and 1937.
Courtesy of Mary Sue Thomas Hill

After leaving South High, Erskine Hill attended OAMC and Oklahoma Unviersity, then embarked on a military career. He became a World War II ace with 127 combat missions in a P-47 and shot down five enemy planes. He later flew 128 combat missions during the Korean War. His assignments have included Deputy Assistant to the Secretary of Defense, Assistant

Deputy Chief of Staff for Plans and Operations, U.S. Air Force, and Commander of the Third Air Force, Commander of the Eighth Air Force, and Commander in Chief, Alaskan Air Command. Here he is congratulated by President Jimmy Carter as he became a four-star general. He was now known as Gen. James E. Hill.
Courtesy of Mary Sue Thomas Hill

Erskine Hill, the future general, was nine when this photograph with his Sunday school classmates was snapped on the steps of the First Church of Christ, Scientist. On the bottom row, far right, he is wearing cap and knickers. With him are Judith Hays, Grace Reece, and Edward Guthrie, and back row, Dick Harbison, Nettie May Huntsberry, unidentified, and Galen Livengood.
Courtesy of Bill Simank

The dome of Alcott School is showing in the right background of this picture of the school that has been known as Stillwater High School, junior high, and middle school. Built in 1921 at 315 West Eighth, it began as a junior high. During the World War II years, it became North High as South High was converted to a junior high school. Then it became a middle school as a new high school was built in 1960. A north wing was added in 1936, an auditorium in 1953, and a cafeteria in 1978. The school closed in 1987 when a new middle school opened on Sangre Road.
Courtesy of Winfrey D. Houston

After the St. Francis Xavier Catholic Church was dedicated in 1902, Father John Heiring began pressing for a school. In 1904, an addition in front of the church served that purpose. In 1919, the parishioners built St. Francis Xavier School (above) next to the church at a cost of $15,433. The school had outside facilities and a hitching place for horses. It remained in use for more than sixty years but was demolished in 1987. In the center, is Father Victor Van Durme, who came to Stillwater in 1914.
Courtesy of George and Lucille Schroeder

From 1922 to 1958, motorists driving
down West Sixth Street headed into what
appeared to be a dead end as they reached
Washington Street and faced Eugene Field
School. The north half of the elementary
school was built in 1922 and the south addition was built in 1928. In 1957, the school
board decided to abandon the site as enrollment declined and commercial development
encroached. Shortly after that it was torn
down and the sharp turn at Washington
was converted to a slight jog. A supermarket
opened on that site on December 23, 1960.
Courtesy of the Sheerar Museum

Washington School at 619 West Twelfth
Street holds memories for hundreds of
Black students who attended there until
Stillwater schools were integrated in 1956.
For years, Washington was a small frame
building. In 1937, the first brick addition
was built and in 1951 it was expanded
again, as shown. Enrollment ranged from
200 to 300, including about 120 grade
pupils. "And they all loved Washington,"
said Mrs. Ruth Haskins Johnson, who
taught there for twenty years. The school
had a complete activities program, including a marching band. Its athletic
teams won many honors. The building in
1988 was being used as quarters for agen-
cies helping low income families, including
Head Start, Action, Inc., and Stillwater
Nursery Center.
Photo by the author

Duck was only a dirt street when Norwood
School was built in the mid-1930s on the
northeast corner of Duck and Miller. The
neighborhood was still sparsely populated
and the three-room brick structure was
built to accommodate children in that
neighborhood. Mrs. Frances Escue was
principal and taught the third and fourth
grades. Mary Hughes taught the first and
second grades. The fifth and sixth grades
were also taught there. The school closed in
about 1938 when Jefferson was remodeled.
It is now the Masonic Lodge.
Courtesy of Shideler's Photo Craft

On May 7, 1972 Stillwater observed Lee Ward Day, honoring the man who spent thirty-one years in the Stillwater school system, seven of them as principal at Washington School. His community contributions included service on boards such as the Stillwater Mission, the YMCA, the Athletic Hall of Fame, Selective Service, Parks and Recreation, Community Chest, the Housing Development, and the Payne-Noble County Housing Authority. His wife, Valerie, was on the city library staff for seventeen years. Lee Ward died March 21, 1982.
Courtesy of the NewsPress

A Call to Worship

Even before the wild run for land on April 22, 1889, church services were held in Stillwater. On Easter morning, the day before the run, G. W. Puckett, a Christian Church minister, called Sooners together on the banks of Stillwater Creek. They sang and prayed, and perhaps gave thanks they had not been caught. And all along the line, where legitimate home seekers awaited the hour, families gathered around covered wagons and tents to worship.

As soon as the dust settled after the run, the town set aside lots for some churches, including North and South Methodist, Presbyterian, Congregational, United Brethren, Christian, and Baptist. Most of the sites were on West Ninth and Tenth streets, since the town center was originally in that area. Some churches started on their assigned lots but soon moved to other locations. The first Catholic Church was several miles east of town and the first Lutheran Church was in the country to the west. Puckett became the first Christian Church minister at Perkins.

The first classes of Oklahoma A&M College began in the Congregational Church in 1891 on the northeast corner of Sixth and Duncan. This was Stillwater's first church. Rev. Richard B. Foster, Congregational's first pastor, was also the first Payne County superintendent of schools.
Courtesy of the Oklahoma State University Library, Special Collections

Presbyterians first met in Stillwater on April 13, 1890 in the Amon Swope Building at Ninth and Main streets. Their first pastor was Simon P. Myers. They organized formally on November 2, 1890, and built their first church, shown here, in the eight hundred block of South Lewis on the west side. Lumber was hauled from Mulhall and members worked nights on the construction. The first services in the new church were held on August 24, 1891. The formal dedication was January 24, 1892. Courtesy of the First Presbyterian Church

The city first assigned lots at Sixth and Duncan to the Presbyterians, but this was open prairie then and members felt they were too far from town. They sold the property, purchased two lots on South Lewis Street for seventy dollars, and built on that site. But in 1907, they changed

their minds again, loaded the church onto a wagon, and moved to Sixth and Duncan where the church has been ever since. The present brick church was dedicated September 14, 1924 on the same site. Courtesy of the First Presbyterian Church

Pioneer families were represented in this Presbyterian Church choir of 1910. Back row, from the left, were Harold Peck, who operated Peck's Lodge, an early Oklahoma A&M College campus hangout; Raymond Moore, whose father, G. E. Moore, founded Stillwater Savings & Loan Association; Loyal Payne; E. J. Smith; A. Frank Melton; and C. E. (Elmer) Donart, for whom the high school built in 1960 was named. Bottom row, from the left were, Emma Bassler, sister of Clarence Bassler; Fearn Hamilton, daughter of Seth Hays Hamilton; Jean Jones; Mrs. Harry B. Bullen, whose husband operated the first lumber yard; Ruth Lahman, daughter of Frank Lahman, who founded the first ice company; and Virginia Fuller.
Courtesy of Bill Simank

Methodists were the first congregation to organize in Stillwater and the second to build a church. Scarcely had the dust settled from the land run of 1889 than Amon W. Swope called the Methodists together for Sunday school and church in his building at Ninth and Main. Members climbed the

outside stairway of the frame building and met on the second floor. In 1892, they built the church above on the southeast corner of Eighth and Duncan. Judge W. H. Wilcox

recorded that J. W. Hubbard was the first minister in Stillwater.
Courtesy of Emma Ingersol Price

119

This is basically the same Methodist
Church built in 1892 after it was remodeled
and covered with brick and stone in 1910.
The building was turned around, enlarged,
and a basement added. It was used as class
rooms for middle school pupils in the early
1920s when Horace Mann School was being
torn down and a new junior high school
was under construction. The Methodists
left this location and dedicated a new
building at Seventh and Duck in 1923.
Courtesy of the H. E. Ricker family

On Friday, November 25, 1892, a group of
Baptists gathered in the two-room frame
school house on Main Street (see photo on
page 108) and organized the First Baptist
Church of Stillwater. Rev. Samuel H.
Huntsberry was in charge. After meeting
in buildings around town, the church, on
July 18, 1896, bought two lots at Ninth and
Duncan. With members doing the work,
the Baptists built the church and dedicated
it on Sunday, September 11, 1898. The
Baptists built a new church at Seventh and
Duncan in 1909. In 1929, this was torn
down and replaced with still another
building. Ground was broken for the
present church sanctuary on December 17,
1950 and worship services were held for the
first time there on May 11, 1952.
Drawing by Sue McGlamery

120

The original First Church of Christ, Scientist, in Stillwater was built in 1895 at the southeast corner of Seventh and Duncan. It was the first west of the Mississippi, the first in the Oklahoma Territory, and the third Christian Science Church in the world dedicated and paid for. In 1927 work began on a new colonial design church that was in use until 1974, when it became the Sheerar Cultural and Heritage Center. The church then moved to its new building of contemporary and rustic design at West Seventh and Ridge Road.
Courtesy of Willis F. Allen, Jr.

Most of the interior of the original First Church of Christ, Scientist was handcrafted by members. The dais and benches were all handmade and some of the benches still exist. In the center is the wood stove and on the right a pump organ, considered very special in the early days.
Courtesy of Willis F. Allen, Jr.

Built in 1893, St. Andrew's Episcopal Church was located at 610 South Duncan where the Strode Funeral Home stands now. The building stayed there until 1922 when it was moved to the northeast corner of Third and Knoblock. It was torn down in 1963 to make way for a contemporary three-building complex still in use. Courtesy of St. Andrew's Episcopal Church

Beautiful early churches gave a touch of elegance to the frontier village of Stillwater. Among them were the First Christian Church on the northeast corner of Seventh and Husband streets, and behind it the South Methodist Church. Christian Church members first worshipped in two frame courthouses before this church was completed in 1898. In 1918, a new brick Christian Church was built on the southwest corner of this same intersection, and on May 11, 1969, the present Christian Church at Duck and Matthews streets was dedicated. Courtesy of the First Christian Church

Without a bishop or a diocese, homesteaders of Catholic faith in Stillwater faced many hardships. For a time starting in 1891 they were served by Father Felix de Grasse from the monastery in Sacred Heart, Oklahoma. In 1896 Stillwater became a mission of Perry and mass was said in Stillwater homes. Finally, in January 1899, parishioners built the above church at a cost of six hundred dollars on a lot at Sixth and West streets. A. M. Greiner built an altar from a packing box. In 1900, Father John Dupret became the first resident priest. Second from right is Father John Heiring.
Courtesy of George and Lucille Schroeder

For this 1906 photo, Stillwater parishioners gathered beside the Catholic church, named for St. Francis Xavier, who was canonized in 1622. Two rooms had been added for priests' quarters, pews were brought in, and the church was dedicated on December 3, 1901. Father John Heiring organized the Altar Society that year and provided for the election of the first parish trustees, A. M. Greiner, H. C. Schaefers, and R. J. Smith.
Courtesy of George and Lucille Schroeder

123

Shortly after the German Evangelical Lutheran Church was incorporated in the Oklahoma Territory in April 1895, Lutherans in the Stillwater area held services in Darnell No. 12 School in the Marena Community eight miles southwest of Stillwater. On September 28, 1897, they purchased land and built their first church, shown here, and called it Friedens Kirche, *which meant "Peace Church." Courtesy of Jene Friedemann*

As Stillwater began to grow, Lutherans moved into or closer to town. In 1912 they purchased the small church at West Ninth and Duncan streets originally built by the Baptists in 1898. The church had now become known as the Evangelical Luthern Friedens (Salem) Church. The original building was destroyed by fire on November 17, 1922 and replaced by this one. Courtesy of Jene Friedemann

Church members flocked to Yost Lake in the early days to watch baptismal services for new converts. When the pavilion filled, onlookers climbed on the roof and on the sliding board. Whether the boats were to be a safety device or to provide a closer view is not known. Yost cabins had not been built at this time. Courtesy of Bill Simank

For nearly a half century starting in about the mid-1920s, the Stillwater Mission provided food, clothing, and sometimes lodging for the needy. The mission started in the above location at about 910 South Main Street. It later moved to Perkins Road and then to 1202 South Fern.
Courtesy of
Mr. and Mrs. Laurence Sinclair

The water backup along Highway 33 near Perkins Corner has been around for years. In 1928, the Stillwater Assembly of God Church used it for baptismal services. This was on the south side of the highway.
Courtesy of
Mr. and Mrs. Laurence Sinclair

Chapter
9

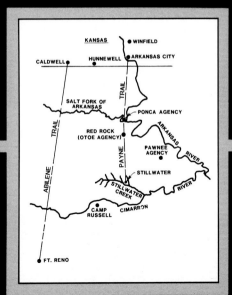

OKLAHOMA A&M COLLEGE— ITS FOUNDING AND MEMORIES

On Monday morning, December 14, 1891, Edward Francis Clark, Stillwater school principal, gathered around him twelve pupils from his highest ranking class. They stood at the door of the Congregational Church, a frame building facing west at the corner of two narrow dirt trails, Sixth and Duncan.

As the church bell clanged, Clark herded the group, along with several other youths, inside. Clark and the pupils were nervous, excited, and neatly dressed. As one of them, James Homer Adams, recalled later, "Not only had we washed our necks, but we had scrubbed behind our ears, and our overalls were freshly washed and ironed."

Inside the youngsters headed in typical fashion to the back of the church. They listened for a time as a man led them in prayer, Bible readings, and what seemed to be a sermon. They fidgeted uneasily and wondered what to do if the offering plate were passed. Then another man pointed to a book on a table in an isolated corner at the front of the room. He told them each would be asked to sign the book and he began to call their names. As young Adams heard his name, he moved shyly near the table and stared at the book. "Do you understand what you are being asked to do?" the stern-looking man asked. "No sir, I don't believe I do," the boy replied. After the man explained the occasion, and as other youths snickered, he wrote his name on the first line of the book. Thus James Homer Adams, age thirteen, became the first registered student at the new Oklahoma Agricultural and Mechanical College.

One by one the others signed the registration book. It now shows that forty-five students registered that day—twenty-three girls and twenty-two boys—but there were fewer than half that many. The others probably were added during the first school year. All of the students were from Stillwater and as far as is known, none had even completed high school. The stern man was Dr. Robert J. Barker, the first president of Oklahoma's new land grant college. He told them they were making history and the greatest opportunity of their lives was knocking on their door.

With him was Dr. James C. Neal, who had come from Florida to teach biology and direct the experiment station. Their own high school principal and teacher, the first in Stillwater, Edward F. Clark, age twenty-five, had now been made one of the first professors in the new college to teach math, history, and English.

Clark had been conducting high school in the Methodist Church. He brought a dozen of his pupils to enroll in the college to make sure enough young people showed up to have classes. To take care of them, the college included a prep school curriculum in its program.

The beginning of classes at Oklahoma A & M College climaxed a struggle begun by the town's pioneers in 1890. By that time, Stillwater's population was about six hundred. Shortly after the Oklahoma Territory was opened to settlement on May 2, 1890, President Harrison signed the Organic Act that provided for organization of the Oklahoma Territory, and he appointed George W. Steele territorial governor.

Steele issued a proclamation on August 5th for an election of a territorial legislature. On August 27th, the new legislature convened. Its tasks included providing for several state institutions, including a land grant college. Such colleges were established as a result of the Morrill Act passed by Congress in 1862 "to teach such branches of learning as are related to agriculture and the mechanical arts."

From the beginning, it was assumed that Stillwater would be the site of one such institution. Its citizens included lawyers, doctors, teachers, and merchants who were vocal and aggressive. They pondered the advantages of locating the state penitentiary, the normal school for teachers, or perhaps the insane asylum in their town. For a fleeting moment, the pioneers considered a daring effort to bring the state capital to Stillwater, but wiser heads prevailed and they decided the nearest to a sure thing was the new land grant college.

Two of Stillwater's representatives to the territorial legislature, both populists, led the fight in Guthrie, then the state capital, to have the college located in Stillwater. James L. Matthews was elected to the House of Representatives and George Gardenhire was elected to a thirteen-member council which corresponded to today's state senate. He was chosen president of the council. Both he and Matthews exerted great influence in the site selection.

Kingfisher, Oklahoma, wanted the state penitentiary, and the two Stillwater delgates bargained with them to get backing for the college. The strongest opposition came from El Reno which also wanted the new land grant school. El Reno's delegate was known to have a penchant for alcohol. Gardenhire and Matthews talked it over with Robert A. Lowry, and on the day the legislature was to decide the site, Lowry gave Frank Ellis, a cowboy from the Z-V Ranch, a ten dollar bill and sent him to see the El Reno delegate. The amount bought enough whiskey to get the delegate intoxicated and he failed to show up for the debate and vote.

On Christmas Eve, 1890, the legislature passed a bill certifying Stillwater as the land grant college site, but the provisions were severe. The town had to raise ten thousand dollars for a new building and two hundred acres for the site of a college and experiment station. El Reno, Kingfisher, and Oklahoma City were standing in line if Stillwater could not put up the money and land. When it became known the new college would get thirty thousand dollars in federal funds, the line became longer.

Stillwater struggled more than a year before it raised the ten thousand dollars. A bond issue passed quickly, 132-0, but was ruled illegal because of the town's low property valuation. Property assessments were immediately raised and a bond issue passed again, but the bonds would not sell at par. Finally, businessmen contributed enough to make up the difference between the bond revenue and the ten thousand dollars.

Getting the land was less complicated. Frank J. Wikoff, a banker and city attorney, was chairman of a committee to solve the problem. He met with Frank E. Duck, Alfred N. Jarrell, Charles A. Vreeland, and Oscar M. Morse, who owned farms on the northwest edge of Stillwater, the favorite site for a college. Duck and Vreeland donated forty acres each. Jarrell and Morse sold forty and eighty acres, respectively, to the city for a nominal sum. The town held a celebration and parade when the college was assured. Other pioneers who played important roles in the Oklahoma Agricultural and Mechanical College effort were Hays Hamilton, Charles Donart, Frank Hutto, Will Swiler, and Charles Knoblock.

Oklahoma A&M College's next milestone was the dedication of its first brick building, Old Central on June 15, 1894. It was originally called the Assembly Building. In the

beginning, heavy emphasis was placed on courses in agriculture, but a department of mechanical engineering was added in 1909 and graduate studies began in 1910.

From these meager beginnings, Oklahoma Agricultural and Mechanical College grew into a major university that emphasized the liberal arts and cultural influences while it remained a leader in agricultural, engineering, business, and veterinary medicine education. In 1957, the state recognized these changes and growth and Oklahoma Agricultural and Mechanical College was given a new name, Oklahoma State University.

Since the Oklahoma Agricultural and Mechanical College graduating class of six in 1896, nearly 140,000 students have earned diplomas. Enrollment in 1987 was 20,112, and the faculty numbered 1,070. Enrollment figures showed that 27 percent of the students were in arts and sciences, 21 percent in business administration and 18 percent in the graduate college. Engineering attracted 14 percent, agriculture, 7 percent, and education and home economics, 6 percent each.

This book is concerned largely with the history of Stillwater. Limited space permits only highlights of history and memories of Oklahoma State University. A thorough and well documented history of the university was written in 1975 by Philip Reed Rulon. It is entitled *Oklahoma State University - Since 1890*, and is available in libraries. A vast twenty-five volume centennial histories series of Oklahoma State University was underway at this writing. It includes histories of the seven colleges, athletics, Old Central, and a centennial year pictorial volume. Those interested in a detailed history of the university will find it in these publications.

The young men fighting to bring a state institution to Stillwater in 1889 called themselves the Vigilantes. Some were so daring they hoped for the state capital. One, Seth (Hays) Hamilton, awakened one night after a dream that Stillwater could have the land grant college. He went to the others in the middle of the night and persuaded them to forget about the other institutions. Hamilton was a member of the school board when the Stillwater system was formally organized in 1891.
Courtesy of Margaret Hays Cross

Oklahoma A&M College's first president, Robert J. Barker, never lived in Stillwater. He staked a claim near Crescent during the land run of 1889 and was afraid to move lest he lose his land. Barker lasted from 1891 until the completion of Old Central in 1894 and then returned to his farm. He was considered an honest administrator but he had difficulties dealing with his faculty and state politicians.
Courtesy of the Oklahoma State University Library, Special Collections

Old Central, the oldest college building in Oklahoma, symbolizes Oklahoma State University to most people. It is a virtual shrine to graduates of every generation. Old Central was the first building erected on the campus after the state legislature established the Oklahoma A & M College in December 1890. Completed in 1894, it was first called the Assembly Building. It housed the first library and several departments. Built on land donated by Frank E. Duck, Old Central cost twenty-five thousand dollars. Courtesy of the NewsPress

A southeast corner entrance graced the campus in the early 1900s. The narrow path and the dirt road made a curve past Williams Hall and Old Central. The dirt road is now University Avenue. The entrance gave way to a campus fire station in 1938.
Courtesy of the Oklahoma State University Library, Special Collections

Theta Pond is a favorite campus relaxation area for students and a fishing hole for youngsters, but in 1894 it was the campus water supply and apparently a watering hole

for cattle. In the right background are Old Central and Williams Hall.
Courtesy of the Oklahoma State University Library, Special Collections

The site of the first boys' dormitory is uncertain. It may have been on the edge of the campus. The six boys in the upper foreground with guitars, banjo, and fiddle

may be the first dance band at Oklahoma A&M College.
Courtesy of the Oklahoma State University Library, Special Collections

Oklahoma A. and M. College
FIRST GRADUATING CLASS
1896

Standing: Homer James Adams, Arthur Wesley Adams, Ervin Greeley Lewis, Oscar M. Morris.
Seated: Alfred Edwin Jarrell, Frank Ellsworth Duck.

**A Great Milestone—
Commencement, 1896**

Each member of the first OAMC graduating class in 1896 made a speech and was presented a bouquet of flowers at Commencement. Seated are left to right, Alfred Edwin Jarrell and Frank Ellsworth Duck, who donated forty acres to get the college started. Standing are James Homer Adams, the first to register in 1891 (his name is incorrect on the plaque), Arthur Wesley Adams, Ervin Greeley Lewis, and Oscar M. Morse.
Courtesy of the Oklahoma State University Library, Special Collections

Only three were in the Oklahoma Agricultural and Mechanical College graduating class of 1897, but among them was Jessica Thatcher, the first woman to receive a degree from an Oklahoma college. Her classmates were George Bower (left), and Andrew N. Caudell. She later taught at Alva and Cleveland and was on the college library staff. Thatcher Hall, a women's dormitory, was named for her.
Courtesy of the Oklahoma State University Library, Special Collections

This muddy bog was campus corner at the turn of the century. The view is looking south on Knoblock from the "jog" near the fire station. A boardwalk appears to have been laid between Third Street and College Avenue, now called University Avenue. It was years before stores, campus hangouts, and even a theatre brightened the corner.
Courtesy of the Oklahoma State University Library, Special Collections

Howard Garfield Seldomridge, an Oklahoma Agricultural and Mechanical College speech professor, traveled to New York in 1908 to realize a dream. He wanted to see Victor Herbert's operetta, The Red Mill. As the cast sang "In Old New York" and members waved their arms wildly, he was inspired. On his return he immediately wrote new lyrics to the song and entitled it "OAMC." It became the official school song.
Courtesy of the Oklahoma State University Library, Special Collections

Oklahoma State University is proud of its baseball teams and their many trips to National Collegiate Athletic Association playoffs, but perhaps no modern team has ever reached the totals shown on this scoreboard after a 1915 game. Cecil Jones, a team member, posed in front of the scoreboard and always contended it was real.
Courtesy of Mrs. Cecil (Helen) Jones

The two most devastating fires in Oklahoma State University history came a few weeks apart in 1914. The first started on Friday morning, August 7, on the third floor of Morrill Hall. The water supply was low during the hot summer, and Morrill was reduced to a rubble. Many college records were destroyed. The picture shows the shell of Morrill while Gardiner Hall on the left was going up in flames on Monday, October 16, 1914. Many students were attired in Halloween costumes as they rushed in to save clothing and furniture in Gardiner, which was then a women's dormitory.
Courtesy of Bill Simank

*John Lester Bishop came to Stillwater in
1904. In town he was known as owner of
Bishop's, a men's clothing store. On the
OAMC campus, however, he was remembered as "Father of the Redskin." In
1909-1910, students wanted OAMC to
have a yearbook but had no funds. Bishop
gave nine hundred dollars to finance the
first Redskin. The 1934 edition was
dedicated to him.*
Courtesy of Irene Ward Bishop

*The towering figure in Oklahoma State
University's one hundred years of existence
is that of Dr. Henry Garland Bennett,
president from 1928 to 1951. He became
president just before the 1929 market crash
and guided the college through the depression, the World War II period, and the great
post-war expansion. His twenty-five-year
plan brought new liberalized curricula,
buildings, and athletic facilities. His leadership provided the transition of Oklahoma
Agricultural and Mechanical College from
what detractors called a "cow college" to a
great university. Dr. Bennett was inducted
into the Oklahoma Hall of Fame in 1938.
Courtesy of the Oklahoma State University
Library, Special Collections*

In 1926 the campus seems bare without the Student Union Building or the fire station. To the far right are stadium bleachers, which existed only on the north side. Thatcher Hall for girls and Hanner for boys face each other across the parade field in front of the campus armory and field house. The street extending through the campus is not Monroe, but Washington, which was then a highway. Just west of it is Whitehurst Hall.
Courtesy of the Oklahoma State University Library, Special Collections

"When I got back from World War II and walked into Swim's, I knew I was home," an Oklahoma Agricultural and Mechanical College veteran said. Generations of students felt that way about the campus hangout at 522 Elm for more than thirty years. Swim's was founded by E. E. Swim and his wife, Adele, in 1921. Their son, Paul, joined them in 1923 and helped manage the place until he retired in 1944. Two other sons, Bustie and Leslie, later became a part of the operation.
Courtesy of Mrs. Paul M. Swim

137

Only an early Oklahoma Agricultural and Mechanical College grad would remember Swim's just as it was in the frame building above. The business started in the house just east of this at 516 Elm, where the E. E. Swims first operated a boarding house. Mrs. Swim was for a time in charge of the Gardiner Hall cafeteria across the street west. Swim's has had several face-lifting jobs since these pictures. It closed not long after the Student Union Building opened.
Courtesy of Mrs. Paul M. Swim

O. R. Brooks' Student Store was a gathering place for many students, especially during the post-World War II years. It was next to the Campus Theatre at 234 South Knoblock, but later moved upstairs across the street on the southeast corner of Knoblock and University.
Courtesy of the Oklahoma State University Library, Special Collections

138

When the Student Union Building was opened in September 1950, student life changed drastically both on and off campus. The union included a bowling alley, a pool and snooker parlor, a restaurant, cafeteria, lounges, and meeting rooms and hotel. As student life centered there, off-campus hangouts began to disappear.
Courtesy of Shideler's Photo Craft

Three first ladies gathered briefly on May 11, 1974, during an historic day at Oklahoma State University. Pres. Richard Nixon had arrived to speak at commencement. Left to right, they are Mrs. Virginia Thomas, wife of Stillwater's mayor, Charles W. (Bill) Thomas; Mrs. Maxine Kamm, wife of Oklahoma State University president Robert B. Kamm; and Mrs. Patricia Nixon, wife of the president. The local women were told to stand on two x's marked on the street and that they would have exactly two minutes to be photographed with Mrs. Nixon.
Courtesy of Mrs. C. W. (Bill) Thomas

Oklahoma State University's official emblem is patterned after a real person. Frank B. "Pistol Pete" Eaton, was the choice of Oklahoma A & M College students to serve as the model after they saw him in an Armistice Day parade in the early 1920s. Eaton died on April 8, 1958, in Perkins, where he spent most of his later years. He was ninety-eight. In his younger days he had been a cowboy, deputy U.S. marshal, and Indian fighter.
Courtesy of the Oklahoma State University Library, Special Collections

Oklahoma Agricultural and Mechanical College's athletic teams and school colors were modeled after those of Princeton in the early days, but in the 1920s the teams became the Cowboys. They replaced their tiger emblem with Pistol Pete, using Frank B. (Pistol Pete) Eaton as a model. Collegiate Emblems, Inc., of Des Moines, Iowa, is credited with creating the emblem in 1923.
Courtesy of the Oklahoma State University Public Information Office

In the beginning of OAMC, a buggy ride around Old Central and Williams Hall was a favorite Sunday afternoon outing.
Courtesy of the Oklahoma State University Library, Special Collections

A 1988 aerial view of the Oklahoma State University campus shows what a difference nearly one hundred years can make. The building with the tower is the library. The more modern building to the right is Oklahoma State University's symbol of the future, the Noble Research Center for Agriculture and the Renewable Natural Resources. When completed the thirty million dollar facility will occupy four acres and is expected to become a world research center for agriculture.
Photo by Gary Lawson, NewsPress

Chapter
10

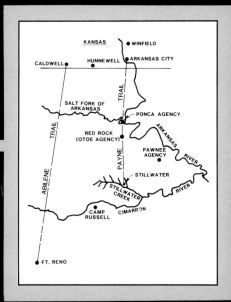

KANSAS ● WINFIELD

CALDWELL●   HUNNEWELL●   ●ARKANSAS CITY

SALT FORK OF
ARKANSAS

TRAIL

PONCA AGENCY

RED ROCK
(OTOE AGENCY)●

ARKANSAS RIVER

PAYNE

PAWNEE
AGENCY
●

●STILLWATER

ABLENE   TRAIL

STILLWATER
CREEK

RIVER

CAMP
RUSSELL
●

CIMARRON

● FT. RENO

GUNFIGHT AT INGALLS—1893

After the Land Run of 1889, the Oklahoma Territory, especially Payne County, became a haven for notorious outlaws. Bill Doolin and the Daltons drifted in and out of Clayton, a small community southwest of Ripley, and when chased by frontier marshals, they often retreated in a hail of gunfire to the Turkey Track Ranch that extended from near present-day Drumright through much of eastern Payne County.

Their favorite hangout, however, was at Ingalls, eleven miles east of Stillwater. There, on the morning of September 1, 1893, occurred the greatest gun battle in the history of the Oklahoma Territory between outlaws and peace officers. It lasted less than a half hour, but before it ended, six persons had been killed and others wounded.

Doolin's gang included such illustrious names as George ("Bitter Creek") Newcomb, ("Dynamite") Dick Clifton, ("Arkansas") Tom Jones, William ("Tulsa Jack") Blake, George ("Red Buck") Waightman, and Charlie Pierce. Most of these had worked as ranch hands with Doolin on the HH spread east of present-day Guthrie or on the Bar-X Ranch in an area called the Triangle where the Cimarron River flows into the Arkansas. Doolin had also worked with the Dalton gang on the Turkey Track Ranch. The men had served apprenticeships in outlawry. When the Daltons were virtually wiped out during the raid on the Coffeyville, Kansas, banks on October 5, 1892, Doolin organized his own gang and soon his reputation as an outlaw exceeded that of the Daltons in the Oklahoma Territory.

Doolin was frequently drawn to Ingalls for a special reason. On March 14, 1893, he married Edith Ellsworth, daughter of J. W. Ellsworth, a Methodist minister and Ingall's second postmaster. The Ellsworths were then living in Lawson, a small community north of Ingalls now known as Quay. After the marriage, Edith worked at the Pierce O. K. Hotel and was a nurse for Dr. D. H. Selph in Ingalls. Doolin brought his gang there often.

In the spring of 1893, Doolin took on another gang member. Bill Dalton decided to abandon Kansas after his brother, Emmett, was sentenced to life imprisonment at Lansing, Michigan. By that summer, Doolin was firmly established as the most wanted outlaw in the territory. The gang's specialties were bank and train robberies.

In July, the gang drifted into Ingalls for another respite. Most of the men stayed at the Pierce O. K. Hotel, but Dalton found quarters at Bee Dunn's ranch east of Ingalls. Although "wanted" posters were displayed throughout the Territory, Ingalls was an isolated community and seemingly a safe haven. Its dreams of becoming the main trade center of the area were already diminishing, although it still boasted two saloons, two livery stables, a drug store, and the Pierce O. K. Hotel.

Five doctors had set up practice in Ingalls, and the post office was established in January 1890 between two of them, Dr. D. H. Selph and Dr. W. R. Call. The town's population had reached about 150 and its businesses were clustered along a two-block stretch of its main street, named Ash. Doolin and his gang caused no trouble at Ingalls. They were friendly with the local citizenry and even contributed to the Methodist Church. They spent most of their time at the Ransom Saloon, the Pierce O. K. Hotel, or at Bee Dunn's ranch.

During the last week in July, Doolin and his gang paid little attention to two new arrivals in Ingalls. The men were Orrington ("Red") Lucas and W. C. ("Dock") Roberts. Ostensibly they came to study the possibility of a rail route to Ingalls. Actually, Roberts was a federal officer and Lucas was a retired federal officer. Word had reached Stillwater that Doolin was in Ingalls. The officers had been dispatched there to gather all possible information on the outlaws and to suggest means of bringing about their capture. Roberts and Lucas made friends with the robbers, drank and played cards with them, and studied their routine. In late August, they reported their findings to Deputy U.S. Marshal John W. Hixon in Guthrie.

On Thursday night, Augsut 31, 1893, two covered wagons moved toward Ingalls, one from Guthrie and one from Stillwater. They appeared as typical Boomer wagons passing by en route to Stillwater for the opening of the Cherokee Outlet on September 16th, but they were loaded with ammunition and deputy marshals. Included among them were Dick Speed, marshal of Perkins, and Tom J. Hueston, former Stillwater city marshal. The plan was to move in on the outlaws in the middle of the night. But one wagon failed to arrive until daybreak and a new strategy was devised.

Dr. J. H. Pickering, one of the first Ingalls doctors, wrote this account of what happened that day:

On the morning of September 1st there was 27 deputy marshals piloted into town in covered wagons. They caused no suspicion as there was hundreds of Boomers moving the same way. 2 wagons stopped at Light's Black Smith Shop & one drove up by my house & they all proceeded to unload in a quiet manner and take positions. Doolan, Bitter Creek, Dynamite Dick, Tulsa Jack, & Dalton was in Ransom & Murry's Saloon. Arkansas Tom was in bed at the Hotel.

Dr. Pickering had overestimated the number of marshals, but he may have included an additional posse rushed from Stillwater to help capture the gang. Dick Speed, driver of one wagon, unloaded his men and weapons west of town. Some hid in the brush. Others took positions behind buildings and trees. Speed then drove his wagon to the front of the blacksmith shop and the O. K. Livery Barn. The other wagon moved to the east edge of town and parked in a grove of trees near Dr. Pickering's house.

Red Lucas and two deputies walked casually into the saloon to check on the outlaws. It was still only 9:00 A.M. They discovered that Arkansas Tom Jones was sick and still in bed at the Pierce O. K. Hotel. Some of the others had switched from drinking to playing poker. Lucas made his report and the marshals made final plans.

As Robert Burns wrote, "The best laid schemes of mice and men gang aft a-gley," and so it was on that morning. Bitter Creek Newcomb left the saloon, mounted his horse and, rifle across saddle, rode slowly down the main street to see his girl friend, Sadie Comley. The officers were not set for action, but Dick Speed interpreted this as meaning the robbers had learned what was going on.

From the door of the O. K. Livery Stable he opened fire on Bitter Creek, and the great Ingalls gunfight was underway. Speed's bullet hit Bitter Creek's rifle, ricocheted off the magazine, and struck Newcomb in the leg. Although wounded, Newcomb fired at least one shot as he fled. Speed was killed almost instantly from bullets fired by Newcomb or from Arkansas Tom Jones, who had risen from his sickbed and was shooting from a hotel window.

After that, the marshals then moved into position near the Ransom Saloon. As their bullets riddled the building, the outlaws slipped out a side door and into the Ransom Livery Barn. Meantime, Del Simmons, a student visiting in Ingalls, was shot and killed as he left the back door of the saloon. The marshals mistook him for an outlaw. Neil Murray, an associate of Ransom's in the saloon, stood at the front door to distract the officers. He was promptly shot in the arm and side. N. A. Walker, a saloon patron, was shot in the liver as he attempted to leave the building.

Tom Hueston had shifted his position from behind a hiding place near the rear of Perry's Dry Good Store to where he could see the saloon entrance. Arkansas Tom Jones had punched a hole in the O. K. Hotel roof and from there he drew a bead on Hueston. He fired twice. One shot hit Hueston in the side and the other in the bowels.

In a matter of moments, still another marshal, Lafe Shadley was mortally wounded. As Dr. J. R. Pickering described the scene:

> By this time the outlaws had got to the stable and saddled their horses. Doolin and Dynamite Dick went out the back door and down a draw southwest. Dalton and Tulsa made a dash from the front door. As they came out Dalton's horse was hit on the jaw & he had a hard time getting him started....He went probely 75 yards when his horse got his leg broke....He got his wire cutters & cut a fence, then got behind one of the other boys and rode off.

Shadley had been pursuing Dalton, and the two exchanged shots. Shadley thought he had hit Dalton. Shadley himself was shot as he ran for cover. The bullet entered his hip and ranged upward to his breast. Another gang member, Dynamite Dick, was shot in the neck as officers sent a hail of bullets at him and Doolin. The latter escaped without a scratch.

With Doolin's departure, Ingalls became silent and the pungent smell of gunpowder hung over the area. One problem still remained. Dr. Pickering was told that Arkansas Tom was still in the O. K. Hotel, probably wounded or killed. He was asked to tend him. Pickering found Jones still in good health, but the outlaw refused to surrender. His Winchester was in his hands and his revolvers were on the bed. When he learned the other outlaws had deserted him, he was deeply hurt. In mid-afternoon he gave himself up.

Young Simmons died at 6:00 P.M. that day. Hueston and Shadley died several days later after being taken to Stillwater for treatment. N. A. Walker died on September 16th. Thus, six persons had been killed, and others wounded in the brief shooting spree. Doolin escaped but his luck ran out on August 24, 1896, when he returned to Lawson to pick up his wife and small son. He was ambushed by a posse headed by famed frontier marshal Heck Thomas and included Dall, Bee, George, and John Dunn. For a time his body was a major attraction while it was on display in a Guthrie store window. He was buried in Summit View Cemetery near Guthrie.

After shooting Doolin, the marshals sighted other members of his gang a few miles away. They were headed for their favorite hide-away, the Turkey Track Ranch. Nearly all of them died in later shoot-outs. Arkansas Tom Jones served a prison sentence and lived to play himself in a movie about the Doolin gang.

The gunfight at Ingalls marked the beginning of the end of bank and train robbing gangs in the Territory. For years the Ingalls community commemorated it with reunions and ceremonies, and in 1938 they erected a monument there to Deputy Marshals Hueston, Shadley, and Speed. Present-day historical tours sometimes include Ingalls and guides recite the story, usually with some embellishment.

INGALLS - ON FRIDAY, SEPTEMBER 1, 1893

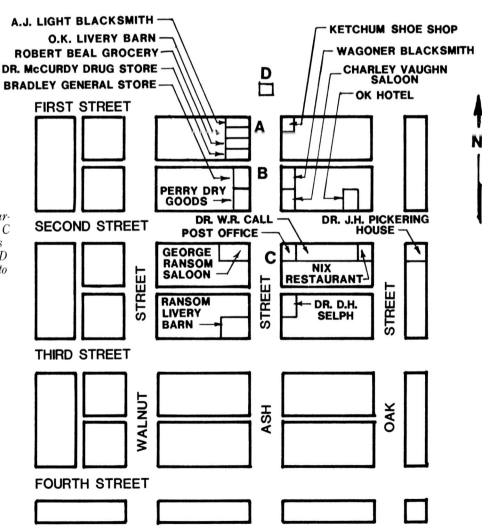

The heaviest action was on Ash Street during the 1893 Ingalls gunfight. A, B, and C on the map show where Deputy Marshals Speed, Hueston, and Shadley were shot. D is where remnants of a monument built to them in 1938 still stand.
Drawing by Dwight Zimbelman

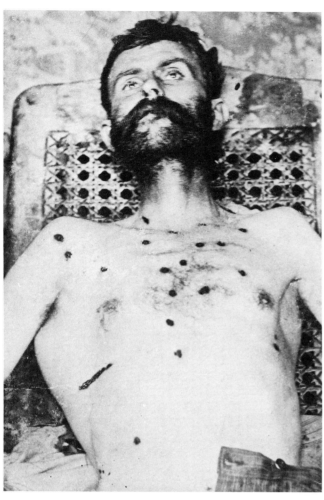

"Go to hell," Bill Doolin shouted at a posse that opened fire on him in the Ransom Saloon at Ingalls. Doolin miraculously escaped the hail of bullets by slipping out a side door, but on August 25, 1896, he was gunned down by a posse when he came back to the Ingalls area for his wife and son. The Stillwater Gazette said he was killed by Rufus Cannon, a half-breed Cherokee who was a member of the posse. His body was for a time on display in a Guthrie store window.
Courtesy of the Western History Collections, University of Oklahoma

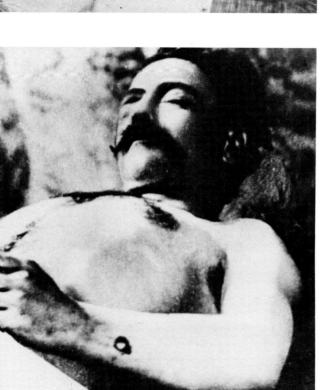

In legend and motion pictures, Rose Dunn, known as Rose of the Cimarron, has been depicted much like this drawing—a gun-toting lover of George ("Bitter Creek") Newcomb who tried to come to his rescue during the Ingalls gunfight. She was actually only fifteen at the time and not Bitter Creek's girl friend. After her death in 1955, her husband Richard Fleming said, "She was a true friend of the outlaws and never betrayed them, but she was never the sweetheart of any." The legends forced Rose to live in seclusion most of her life.
Drawing by Mike Parks, courtesy of the Oklahoma Press Association

George ("Bitter Creek") Newcomb caught the first bullet fired at Ingalls, but escaped and recovered. On the night of May 1, 1895, he and his crony, Charlie Pierce, returned to the Dunn Ranch near Ingalls and were riddled with bullets. One account credited a posse with shooting them. Another said Bee Dunn shot them to gain a meager reward while the two were lying down.
Courtesy of the Oklahoma Territorial Museum, Oklahoma Historical Society

147

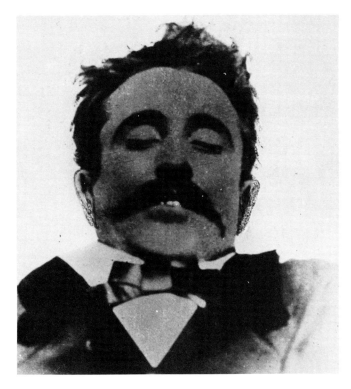

William Blake, alias Tulsa Jack, had worked with Bill Doolin as a ranch hand on two ranches in the Oklahoma Territory before their crime spree began. Blake also escaped the Ingalls gunfight unscathed, but he was killed in another shoot-out with a posse after he and other Doolin gang members held up a train in Dover, Oklahoma. His body was also displayed at Guthrie. *Courtesy of the Western History Collections, University of Oklahoma*

Dr. D. H. Selph gave medical aid to Lafe Shadley and others wounded at Ingalls. Bill Doolin's wife was a nurse for Dr. Selph for a time before the gunfight. Selph later moved to Stillwater and set up practice in the one hundred block of West Seventh Street. The Selph Building is now on the National Register of Historic Landmarks. *Courtesy of the Selph family*

For a time it appeared that Roy Daugherty, alias Arkansas Tom Jones, would be the only member of the Doolin gang to die of natural causes. After his capture at Ingalls, he served a prison term and then lived to play himself in a movie about Doolin. He even traveled with the show. He apparently became bored and returned to his old ways. He was shot and killed by police on August 16, 1924 in Missouri, while a fugitive from a bank hold-up. *Courtesy of the Guthrie Territorial Museum*

Harry Selph was only seven and playing marbles in Ingalls main street when Dick Speed opened fire on Bitter Creek Newcomb. His father, William B. Selph, had always told him when he heard gunfire, which was often in Ingalls, to run for the cellar. When shots rang out on September 1, 1893, Harry jumped over a fence more than three feet high and went feet first into the cellar, which was already crowded. Harry's uncle was Dr. D. H. Selph. He is shown here years later as co-owner of the Model Grocery.
Courtesy of the Selph family

Famed frontier U.S. Marshal Heck Thomas organized and led the posse that killed Bill Doolin on August 25, 1896. Doolin had been captured in Eureka Springs, Arkansas on January 15, 1896, but made a daring escape from jail at Guthrie on July 5. In August, he rode into the Lawson (Quay) area, hopeful of slipping away with his wife and son. On Tuseday night, August 25, Doolin rode ahead of a wagon carrying his wife, son, and their belongings. Confronted by Thomas and the posse, he refused to surrender and was riddled with bullets.
Courtesy of the Western History Collections, University of Oklahoma

Vandals and erosion have almost destroyed a monument built in 1938 to honor the three deputy marshals slain there. These remnants are at the north end of Ash Street, which has also virtually disappeared. *Photo by the author*

Bee Dunn's grave marker still stands tall in the center of the Ingalls cemetery, although citizens protested his burial there in 1896 and scattered hog entrails on his grave. A former crony of the Doolin gang, Dunn was in the posse that killed Doolin and was accused of being a party to the killing of two other gang members, George ("Bitter Creek") Newcomb, and Charlie Pierce. Dunn received a thirty-six dollar reward for his participation in the ambush of Doolin. *Photo by the author*

150

Roland H. Selph holds a gold Elgin watch that outlaw Bill Doolin gave his father, Dr. D. H. Selph, shortly after the Ingalls gunfight. Doolin was grateful when Dr. Selph amputated a toe badly mangled with buckshot. During the operation, Doolin lay on a table in the back of Bill Selph's grocery. The house above is what's left of the O. K. Hotel from which Arkansas Tom Jones opened fire on U.S. deputy marshals. The hotel was moved to Stillwater in about 1902 and these remnants are now at 812 South Hester.
Photo by the author

On his tombstone in Summit Cemetery on the northeast edge of Guthrie are the words, "William 'Bill' Doolin, 1858-1896, Killed August 25, 1896 Near Lawson, Oklahoma Territory by Deputy United States Marshal Heck Thomas and Posse." Doolin's grave was in an isolated spot but in 1977, the body of another outlaw, Elmer McCurdy, was brought to Guthrie from California and interred beside him. McCurdy had been killed by a posse in Osage Hills on October 7, 1911.
Photo by the author

Chapter 11

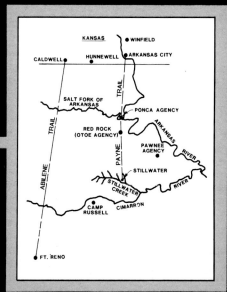

GOODBYE STILLWATER, HELLO CHEROKEE STRIP

After achieving triumph after triumph in gaining a townsite, the county seat, and a college, Stillwater faced a major dilemma in 1893. In one minute's time, it lost half its population. On April 22, 1889, about three hundred settlers had rushed pell-mell southward into the Stillwater Valley area. By the summer of 1893, the population had grown to nearly 1,200 but 600 townspeople gathered at the same line as the Land Run of 1889 on the outskirts of Stillwater and rushed north, this time into the Cherokee Outlet.

The Outlet extended along the Kansas-Indian Territory border for about two hundred miles. It was part of a land package the Cherokees received in 1827 to provide them a permanent corridor to hunting grounds in the west. Its total area was about seven million acres. The Outlet lands were considered the richest, most desirable in the Territory. Since the 1889 Land Run, a constant clamor had risen to open them to settlement.

For fifteen years the coveted land had been occupied and controlled by cattlemen who had organized as the Cherokee Strip Livestock Association. The group opposed opening the unoccupied lands to homestead settlement, and David L. Payne considered it the most formidable opponent of his Boomer movement. Finally, on May 19, 1893, the Cherokee Nation relinquished its claim to the lands for $8,595,750. On August 19th, President Grover Cleveland issued a proclamation opening the Outlet and surplus lands of the Tonkawas and Pawnees for settlement at noon on September 16, 1893.

The excitement that swept through the Oklahoma Territory and Kansas was greater than that during the time of the Run of 1889. By early September from fifty thousand to seventy thousand land hungry had arrived on the southern Kansas border. Stillwater and Orlando became the gathering points for thousands on the southern border of the Outlet. Others assembled on the east and west.

Stillwater's own people were caught up in the movement and many prepared to run for a free homestead in the rich Outlet lands. "On to the Cherokee Strip" had replaced "On to Oklahoma" as the cry. Nearly all settlers referred to the land as "The Strip," rather than the Outlet, although the actual Cherokee Strip was a small band of land about two-and-a-half miles wide that once extended along the Kansas border. A special emissary from Washington reported from Stillwater that the craze for Strip property was so great that in all likelihood Chandler, Perkins, and Stillwater would be depopulated by the run.

Soon a carnival atmosphere prevailed. Land seekers on fast ponies practiced daily from the edge of Stillwater to the line from which the run would be made. This would be between Cherokee and Ranch streets today. Beside them were young men pedaling feverishly who had decided to make the run on bicycles. The cyclists had formed an organization. Some were from Chicago and others were from Ohio. They practiced daily on the roughest terrain, hoping it would prepare them for the rugged run.

Lawyers who specialized in land problems arrived in town daily. They hoped that quarrels betwen settlers or between settlers and the government would bring them clients. On the trains into the Territory came a swarm of gamblers and confidence men. They worked on the streets and in the wagon camps fleecing settlers with all sorts of devices and games. Now and then cowboys brought in fleet ponies and auctioned them off in the camps. And in the midst of all were the hated Sooners. Said an article in the Perkins *Bee.*

Now, the sooner is looked upon as a thief. He steals across the line before the hour of opening and hides in the brush or ravine and squats on a claim just about the time or a few minutes after the opening hour. The honest home-seeker may make a twelve or fifteen mile run for that particular quarter and then find a sooner has been sitting there for an hour. Of course the law deals roughly with the sooner, but how is one to get evidence against him?

Another type of land swindler had also moved onto the Outlet borders. These individuals moved from one land run to another. They staked claims, held them for awhile, and then sold them at an inflated price. The Arkansas *Traveler* estimated there were two thousand such people ready to move into the Outlet. To thwart them, President Cleveland set aside a strip of land one hundred feet wide all around the Outlet. He ordered booths set up at nine points. Those seeking homesteads would have five days to register for the run. After the run, those on the land would have to produce a registration slip. Those who had already used up their eligibility at previous land runs would be disqualified. Stillwater was chosen as the site for one booth, which brought thousands of home seekers into town.

In some ways, things would be much better for the homesteaders for this run than they were in 1889. Many had rushed to stake claims that year and then suffered for lack of water. Now, wells were being dug in all potential town sites so there would be ample water supply for people and animals. Twenty former packing house butchers from Chicago moved into the Outlet from the north. They occupied five rail cars, one full of horses. Another car contained thirty-five tents. The butchers intended to scatter through the Outlet and stake claims in the important townsites and promptly open meat markets. Meantime, the government had already made plans to establish post offices immediately following the run. The first postmasters had already been selected.

As September 16th neared, rumors spread all along the line. Some said the run would have to be made on foot—that all wagons and ponies would have to remain behind. Another said trains would be barred in the Outlet the day of the run or they would be permitted to travel only five miles an hour. In spite of the rumors, those bent on winning a claim continued to buy good saddles and horses and train the animals to run a long distance.

At high noon, September 16, 1893, the big moment finally arrived. Soldiers with guns cocked and ready to fire the starting signal were spaced at intervals along the line. An accidental gunshot sent some homesteaders across the line eight minutes early. Other soldiers then started firing and the line moved like a giant wave into the Cherokee Outlet. That evening, as the dust from the run settled, Stillwater's population was only half what it had been on September 15th.

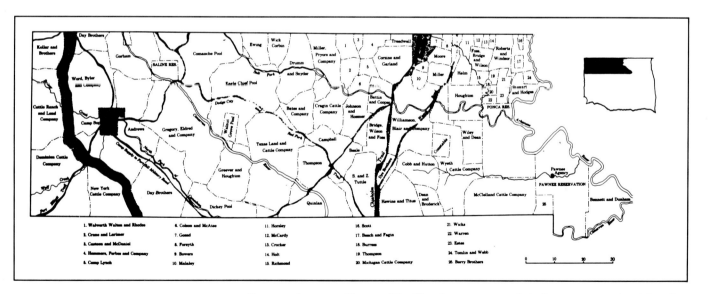

For several years, cattlemen of the Cherokee Strip Livestock Association held a monopoly on lands in the Cherokee Outlet through leases obtained from Indians. They sought to keep others out and opposed David L. Payne's Boomer movement. The map shows leaseholders in the Outlet; the small state map, upper right, shows the Outlet as part of the state. The government broke up the monopoly in January 1892 when it bought the Outlet from the Cherokees and made plans to open it for white settlement. From Historical Atlas of Oklahoma, *by John W. Morris, Charles R. Goins, and Edwin C. McReynolds. Copyright 1965, 1976, 1986 by the University of Oklahoma Press*

Hopeful settlers in covered wagons gathered for the Cherokee Strip run at Stillwater. Automobiles were not yet a part of the mainstream, so settlers brought all types of wagons and horses. Some shipped in racing *thoroughbreds to get ahead in the race, but these could not compete with the small cow ponies accustomed to roving the prairies. A few decided to try bicycles and others were ready to make the run on foot. By the time* *of the opening, between twenty and thirty thousand people had gathered.*
Courtesy of the Archives and Manuscripts Division, Oklahoma Historical Society

Tents about fourteen by twenty feet in size were set up at fifty points along the borders of the Cherokee Strip for advance registration. The government hoped these would keep Sooners from illegally staking claims *as they did in the Run of 1889. People were from all walks of life. Lawyers, doctors, gamblers, the rich, the poor were in the throng that gathered to register. Each registrant was given a ticket he would later have* *to produce when he filed his official claim at the land office.*
Courtesy of the H. E. Ricker family

Many Stillwater residents were in this long line to register. Some had made the 1889 Run south into the Stillwater Valley. Now, almost half the town's population was being lured to make the run northward into the strip. The town's population was about twelve hundred in 1893. J. H. Swope estimated this line to be three-fourths of a mile long. At times there were as many as four such lines. When the booths closed in the evening, many of the settlers stayed in line all night to keep from losing their places. Courtesy of the H. E. Ricker family

Five riders, including J. H. (Harry) Swope of Stillwater, were employed to "ride the line" and keep order. The weather was hot and dry and the horses kicked up dust that drifted over the long lines. Drinking water was at a premium and was hauled from half a mile away. Some in the line took drinks or food into the registration tents and offered them to clerks in exchange for the favor of registering early. Often they were successful. The riders worked nights, too, as the settlers became restless. Swope said the government never paid him or the others for their week of work.
Courtesy of the Oklahoma State University Library, Special Collections

On the day of the land run, the masses of humanity move closer to the starting line. The man in the foreground holds them back as they await the signal. Hot south winds, clouds of dust, and nervous, frightened horses cause great unrest. Soldiers with carbines are stationed every six hundred yards ready to give the starting signal. Courtesy of the H. E. Ricker family

*This historic photo captures the beginning of the Cherokee Strip Land Run. The noon starting time was forgotten when a nervous cavalryman accidentally discharged his rifle eight minutes early. As the settlers charged across the line, others saw the cloud of dust and followed suit.
Courtesy of the Archives and Manuscripts Division, Oklahoma Historical Society*

Covered wagons, buggies and the train get the run underway on the southern line of the Strip. Settlers jammed the rail cars and even stood on the top of the train. The government had already laid out townsites and towns born that day included Perry, Ponca City, and Tonkawa. The Santa Fe Railroad reported it sold twelve thousand tickets in one day as people mobbed the depot. The wiser settlers may have been those who stepped a few feet across the line and staked claims. Theirs turned out to be among the best.
Courtesy of the H. E. Ricker family

In spite of precautions, the Sooners proved to be a curse in the 1893 run. We could see smoke from the great prairie fires that had been set by Sooners, who had sneaked in earlier, to retard the progress of the oncoming settlers," reported Clarence Bassler, pictured here. One woman was burned to death in a fire set by Sooners. Bassler's father was gone for ten days after the land run before his family heard from him.
Courtesy of the NewsPress

A special ceremony marking the line from which both the Cherokee Strip Run of 1893 and the Land Run of 1889 were made was held April 10, 1960 at the Stillwater airport. George Shirk, president of the Oklahoma Historical Society, addressed a group of 89'ers and two thousand others. To his left is Dr. B. B. Chapman. The historical marker in the background is now between Cherokee and Ranch streets on Highway 177. The line is now in Stillwater's city limits.
Courtesy of Dr. B. B. Chapman

159

Chapter
12

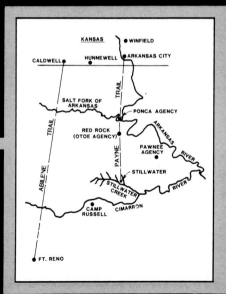

THE COUNTRY YEARS—1917-1945

After early struggles laid the foundation for the future, Stillwater remained a quiet country town for nearly thirty years. The population in 1917 as World War I began was nearly 3,000. By 1930, the number had grown to only 7,016, and as World War II approached, Stillwater boasted a few more than 10,000 residents.

This chapter seeks to capture the history and flavor of the country years. They began with the dark days of World War I. The people put aside all other concerns during 1917 and 1918 and gave total suport to the war effort. Life centered around the War House near Eighth and Main, built especially in 1917 for home front headquarters. Patriotic fervor was at a peak. Downtown parades and rallies around M. G. Searcy's Grocery at Seventh and Main were frequent.

After the war ended in November 1918, Stillwater settled into a quiet, country-town existence. It remained thus through World War II. Ask citizens who lived there during this period and they will tell you the following are among their lasting memories of that era: merchants whose stores reflected a real country flavor, first Orlando Eyler, Will Swiler, Sam Miller, and Jake Katz, and then Ben Cooksey, Peyton Glass, Sr., John L. Bishop, Glenn Douglas, O. V. Mullendore, and others...farmers sitting along curbs and on the courthouse lawn...everybody coming to town on Saturday night...downtown hotels—the Nichols, Youst, and Commercial—then the Going, Grand, and Rains...no traffic lights...many dirt streets and the edges of town at Washington and the railroad tracks...schools, especially South High, close to town and all the kids walking...soda fountains in all drug stores...Doc Whittenberg...boarding houses with college kids paying twenty-five dollars a month for board and room...downtown coffee houses where friends clustered twice a day...Crystal Plunge...dime

stores on Main Street...Safeway, C. R. Anthony, and J. C. Penney stores all downtown...doctors downtown in upstairs offices...and noisy tent revivals.

The country years ended much as they began, with war threatening not only the national security but the community's economic survival as well. World War II placed Oklahoma Agricultural and Mechanical College in dire straits as many of its male students joined the armed forces. Since Stillwater's cconomy was largely dependent on the college, its survival became the primary concern apart from the war itself. The town and college joined together to cope with the problem.

In January 1942, a month after the Japanese attack on Pearl Harbor, a War Activities Committee headed by Roy T. Hoke went into action. Its members were Dr. Henry G. Bennett, Oklahoma Agricultural and Mechanical College president; Mayor L. E. McConkey, C. R. (Robert) Bellatti, publisher of the *NewsPress*, Charles ("Elmer") Donart and Ralph Archer, president and manager of the Chamber of Commerce, respectively; Phil Wilber, and Claude Bradshaw.

For several months, Dr. Bennett, Hoke, Bellatti, and Wilber ran shifts to Washington calling on military leaders and congressmen. Their aim was to convert Oklahoma Agricultural and Mechanical College into a war training center. Their success exceeded their fondest dreams. With the help of Senator A. S. (Mike) Monroney, they brought to Oklahoma Agricultural and Mechanical College twelve training programs that involved nearly 40,000 service men and women. The W.A.V.E.S. (Women's Reserve of the U.S. Naval Reserve) Naval Training School was the largest, with 10,783 participants. Another naval training school brought 6,700 men to Oklahoma Agricultural and Mechanical College. Army and civilian programs added thousands more.

Quonset huts sprung up on campus. The college built barracks along West Sixth in the area now occupied by the Stillwater Medical Center. The vast operation tided the college and the city through critical times and served as a base for a dynamic postwar period.

The "War House," built in the middle of East Eighth Street just off Main between the Youst Hotel and the Stillwater National Bank, became headquarters for Stillwater's World War I home front effort. Citizens of all ages rallied to the cause starting in 1917. War bonds and savings stamps were sold there, and the house was a center for patriotic rallies.
Courtesy of the NewsPress
Pierce Collection

A 1917 view of Main Street during a patriotic parade shows the War House in the middle of Eighth Street sandwiched between the Youst Hotel and the Stillwater National

Bank. The Model-T leading the parade is sagging under the load of soldiers, weapons, and ammunition. In the background are M. G. Searcy's Grocery and Katz Depart-

ment Store which is still in the building second from corner.
Courtesy of James and Pearl Todd

A close look at this 1917 picture suggests everyone has gone home from the parade except the photographer, who snapped a remarkable night shot amid the rain and lightning. The little War House is silhouetted behind the street light glare next to the Youst Hotel. The Camera theatre lights are still glowing.
Courtesy of the Sheerar Museum, Jaycee Scrapbook, 1954

A portable generator with steam engine on the back was probably brought in by the circus to generate power for its operation. The generator was mounted on a truck chassis with solid tires. This picture was taken about the time of the 1924 circus.
Courtesy of the NewsPress, *Pierce Collection*

In its glory days, starting as early as 1906, the Stillwater station had six passenger trains with connections to Oklahoma City, Tulsa, Kansas City, the Panhandle, and other points. This picture shows citizens meeting the train in 1917. Limited passenger service continued until the mid-1950s when the Perkins train station was torn down and some track taken up. Stillwater currently has freight service from Perry via Pawnee largely to serve industries along Perkins Road.
Courtesy of the NewsPress
Pierce Collection

Train service, both passenger and freight, was still going strong in 1940, when this crew was running the Stillwater station. Crew members standing, from left, are Walter McDonald, agent; Roy Cundiff, operator; Jesse Ham, chief clerk; and W. D. Bentley, cashier. McDonald was the agent at the A. T. & S. F. Stillwater Station from 1908 to 1948.
Courtesy of Lawrence Gibbs

A view of West Seventh from Main Street in 1917 shows a parade of homefront volunteers. Both corner buildings had outside stairways then. The new courthouse is visible in upper right. The Pioneer Telephone and Telegraph Company was at 702 South Main and getting ready to change its name to Southwestern Bell. On the north side of Seventh is the office of abstractor J. E. Sater, who reconstructed many courthouse records after the fire of 1894.
Courtesy of the NewsPress,
Pierce Collection

Is this Charlie Chaplin leading a parade down Main Street in 1917? Take a second look. His fans say it is probably someone made up like him. Whoever it is looks rather grim, while the clowns and others seem to be enjoying the merriment. Old timers say all are probably heading for the Opera House for a Chaplin show.
Courtesy of the NewsPress,
Pierce Collection

Stillwater's early banks usually clustered around the corner of Eighth and Main streets, but one ventured north to the southwest corner of Seventh and Main. The Stillwater State Bank started in 1918, but lasted only four years before merging with the State Bank of Commerce. It was not associated with the earlier Stillwater State Bank started by Shelly W. Keiser. The crowd outside is reminiscent of those that gathered around banks during the 1932 bank holiday.
Courtesy of the NewsPress,
Pierce Collection

Parades were frequent in 1918 and this one is crossing Main and moving east on Ninth. On the right is the Model Grocery, owned first by H. E. Wilson in 1915 and by Harry and Earnest Selph starting in about 1926. Their father, William B. Selph, was a gro-
cer in Ingalls at the time of the 1893 gunfight. The Selphs moved to Stillwater and established a store, first on the corner of Seventh and Main where Katz was later located, then a few doors south of there. Still later they took over the Model Grocery.
Across the street to the west in center of photo is the former Swope building, still two-story, and in the background is the dome of Alcott School.
Courtesy of the NewsPress,
Pierce Collection

The first savings and loan association in Stillwater opened in May 1920 on the second floor of what later became known as the Hoke Building. George E. Moore was principal founder of Stillwater Savings and Loan. The first secretary-treasurer was Charles Bartholomew. As the association grew, it moved about 1926 to the location shown here at 113 West Eighth. It remained there for thirty-nine years and in 1965 built modern facilities at 601 South Husband. In August 1985, Stillwater Savings and Loan added a new facility with drive-in services at Boomer and Duck streets.
Courtesy of Mrs. Virginia Bills

Stillwater's second power plant was built about 1920 and is remembered largely for the towering smoke stack added in 1928. It was just off Fourth Street near the site of the first plant. The plant and smoke stack were demolished in 1983.
Courtesy of the Sheerar Museum,
Jaycee Scrapbook, 1954

168

'Doc' Whittenberg and His Hospitals

Dr. William Claton Whittenberg started practice in Morrison in 1900. His first operation was on young John Frank for a hernia. The doctor took the door off his office and used it as an operating table. Whittenberg came to Stillwater in 1911 and for a time performed operations at his home at 404 South Duck. In about 1917, he rented the former Linden Hotel building, shown here, on the southeast corner of Ninth and Lewis and it became Stillwater's first hospital.
Courtesy of Katherine Gessler Bandelier

Dr. W. C. Whittenberg found the Linden Hotel unsuited for good medical care. In 1920, Adam Focht, who had struck it rich in oil, offered to finance a new one, and Whittenberg happily accepted. The second Whittenberg hospital, above, was built at
Eighth and Lewis where the Municipal building now stands. Whittenberg was the only staff doctor. His ambulance was a Model-T ford operated by his maintenance man.
Courtesy of the NewsPress,

Dr. W. C. Whittenberg is remembered most by this picture. He loved hunting and owned several dogs. During the depression, another Stillwater physician chided him for not collecting from patients. "Get it while there are tears in their eyes," he advised. "But," said Whittenberg's nurse of fifteen years, Anna Frank Ferguson, "Dr. Whittenberg knew they were hard up and he felt sorry for them. He often never charged them anything."
Courtesy of Anna Ferguson

A staff of eight nurses helped Dr. Whittenberg operate the hospital. They were, left, Maude Brower, Beaulah Roether, Edith Olmstead, Katherine Geller Bandelier, Harriet Kaiser Barnes, Juanita Geller, Ethel McPherson, and Leota Amick. When all were stricken during the 1918 flu epidemic, citizen volunteers flocked in to help.
Courtesy of Katherine Gessler Bandelier

When Dr. W. C. Whittenberg moved his hospital from Ninth and Lewis to the eight hundred block of Lewis in 1920, the building was remodeled and made into the Rex Hotel and Apartments. It had originally been the Linden Hotel.
Courtesy of the City of Stillwater

If you liked black and touring cars, the place to go in 1917 was Charles C. Platt's Ford Agency on the southwest corner of Eighth and Husband streets. Bodies and chassis of Fords were shipped separately. Drivers took the train to Oklahoma City, then sat on the gas tank of a car as they drove the chassis to Stillwater. Ford bodies came to Stillwater on freight cars and were mounted locally. In the background is the Methodist Church when it was on Eighth. Beyond that are Alcott and Horace Mann schools. The car in the foreground is offering taxi service.
Courtesy of C. W. ("Bill") Thomas

Stillwater's first motor home made its appearance in 1921. Charles C. Platt, Ford dealer, built the body on a Model-T chassis. It had beds, curtains, a coal oil stove, and even a limited bathroom facility. Platt's son, H. J., was standing by the vehicle. Courtesy of Charles E. Platt

A Whippet that could go from 0 to 55 miles per hour in thirty seconds and get thirty miles per gallon of gas, the Willys Knight, and the luxury Willys Overland were all a part of Clarence E. Hull's inventory in the early 1920s. Hull first operated the agency in partnership with Frank C. Schedler at 722 South Main but his garage above is at 116 East Sixth. Courtesy of Mrs. Fay Hull

Richard Stanley Ward came to Stillwater from Seiling in 1921 and at first was associated with Grover Shideler's Jewett-Graham Paige Agency. When General Motors took over production of Chevrolets in 1924, Ward opened his own agency at Ninth and Husband streets in the former A. W. Sollers Livery Barn. He moved from there to 113 East Ninth and then in 1934 he built the above building at Eighth and Lewis that for thirty years housed Ward Chevrolet. Courtesy of Irene Ward Bishop

After working for Richard Stanley Ward for two years, Judson Bryan in 1937 joined Forrest E. Barnett in a Studebaker agency in the one hundred block of East Sixth. A short time later the two switched to Oldsmobile. Bryan purchased Barnett's interest in the agency and in 1988 had operated for fifty years on the site above which had originally been Clarence E. Hull's Whippet Agency. Courtesy of J. P. Bryan

A team of white horses pulls a Fresno across Husband Street during paving of the seven hundred block in about 1923. In the background is the steam powered cement mixer. On the right is Grover Shideler's Dodge-Plymouth Agency and rising above it in the background is the top of Hoke Building. The Fresnos were used to move dirt and to smooth the terrain.
Courtesy of Iva May Sherwood

Theodore Gudgel and Harry McVay, possibly Stillwater's first paving contractors, have their mixing machine near the corner of Eighth and Husband. The machine's long arm is funneling concrete to the *workers. On the right is the site where the Stillwater post office was moved in 1933. The brick building on the corner to the south has been the site of Charles C. Platt's Ford agency, the Farmers Co-op Grocery,* *Payne County Creamery, Marvin Flaming's Foodliner, and the Stillwater Laundry. It is now a parking lot.*
Courtesy of Iva May Sherwood

The fire department's first ladder truck with hard rubber tires all around was almost homemade. The town bought the chassis and then built the ladder equipment. In the mid-1920s, it is shown parked on East Ninth Street almost in front of that familiar landmark, the Opera House. Courtesy of the Stillwater Fire Department

The Stillwater National Bank opened for business in these new quarters in 1925, still at Eighth and Main streets. The post office moved that year from the nine hundred block of South Main to the back of the bank building. It was the seventh post office loca-tion. The post office moved again to Eighth and Husband streets in 1933, but the bank remained here until 1967 when it built a new modern bank at 608 South Main. Photograph by William E. Bell, Courtesy of Shideler's Photo Craft

175

The third version of the First National Bank was completed in 1924. Through the Country Years, the two banks faced each other across Eighth and Main streets. In 1964, First National built its present modern building on this same location, 808 South Main.
Courtesy of the Sheerar Museum.
Jaycee Scrapbook, *1954*

The Katz Store had an informal appearance through the Country Years. Jake Katz moved from the west side of Main in 1913. He was at first in the building second from the corner but expanded to Seventh Street when the Selph family moved their grocery store to Ninth and Main. Some said this store front reminded them of the Alamo. A pool hall and later a dance hall were on the second floor.
From The Redskin, *1948*

Jake Katz went to his store every day and even in his eighties greeted customers at the door. One of his memorable sales was a pair of trousers belonging to outlaw Bill Doolin in 1896. Katz always learned his customer's names and could call several generations of a family by first names. He always carried a pocketful of suckers for children. "They'll remember us when they grow up," he said. Jake Katz died July 2, 1968 shortly before his ninety-fifth birthday.
Courtesy of the NewsPress,

176

The Douglas Food Market of the 1920s
resembled Orlando M. Eyler's store of the
1890s. It was long before frozen foods and
self-service. Glenn Douglas made eight
deliveries a day. His work day was
eighteen hours. He dressed his own
chickens and moved from the corner in
the 1950s as complaints arose about
feathers blowing on Main Street. Douglas
is in left foreground above. In the sweater
at right is Mrs. C. H. McElroy.
Courtesy of Glenn Douglas

In 1926, Walter E. Going's new hotel was
billed as Stillwater's "principal hotel and
headquarters for the traveling man."
Rooms with bath were $2.25 a night, but
only $1.25 without bath. The Going Hotel
had sixty rooms, half of them with bath.
The Blue Willow Lunch operated in connec-
tion with the hotel. The Going was located
in the one hundred block of West Seventh on
the north side. It has now been converted
into an office building.
Courtesy of
Mr. and Mrs. Lyle H. Winterhalter

**A Cowboy Band Finds
Fame in the Cities**

*Otto Gray became Stillwater's nation-
ally known entertainer in 1926. His cowboy
band became as well known as many big
name popular bands as he performed on
national radio networks and major radio
stations.* Billboard *was among publications
that paid tribute to Gray. Gray was born
March 2, 1884, and came to Payne County
in 1889 with his parents, who homesteaded
north of Mehan.*
Courtesy of the NewsPress,

*A fleet of Cadillacs and the big LaSalle
shown on the right provided transportation
for Otto Gray's band. His travel budget
averaged one hundred thousand dollars a
year as the band performed coast-to-coast.
One of Gray's close friends was the Duke of
Paducah, comedian of the Grand Ole Opry,
who visited Gray in his Stillwater home.*
Courtesy of the NewsPress,

Otto Gray's band consisted largely of this group; left to right, Ernest Bevins, Lee Allen, Chief Sanders, Wade (Hy) Allen, Owen Gray (Otto's son), Florence Powell Gray (Otto's wife), who was always called "Mommie," Otto, and Rex, who was billed as "The Wonderful Police Dog," and the "bark of the air." Rex barked to the rhythm of the music during radio shows.
Courtesy of Mrs. Jim (Ruth) Wells

Billboard *hailed Otto Gray's band as "the nation's original cowboy band," but it wasn't. In 1924, George Youngblood, a Ripley business man, and Frank Sherrill, a fiddler and oil worker, put together the first band. As it attracted attention, they brought in as front man colorful Billy McGinty, a former Teddy Roosevelt Rough Rider and performer with Buffalo Bill. Their group became Billy McGinty's Cowboy Band. When the demands for performances became too great, McGinty and the others turned the band over to Otto Gray. He reorganized, added new personnel, and achieved national fame. Band members are, front row, left to right, an unidentified woman and child, Mrs. Billy (Mollie)*

McGinty, Billy McGinty, Paul Sharum, and Ulys Moore. In the back row are Harry Hackney, Frank Sherrill, Roy Munday, Guy Messecar, and Paul Harrison. Seated in front is Ernest Bevins.
Courtesy of Marie Sherrill Rainwater

179

A familiar face (and voice) in Stillwater's business district for half a century was Forrest Boaz, on the right, in his first establishment at Sixth and Main streets on the site later occupied by the Grand Hotel and the Stillwater National Bank. "Bozie" specialized first in saddles and harnesses and was later known for his craftsmanship in canvas work and car upholstery until his death in 1968. He was a founder of both state and Stillwater American Legion organizations. The car has a 1927 tag.
Courtesy of Forrest K. Boaz

In 1929, forty years after the land run, the Stillwater Valley had largely yielded to homes, businesses, and farms. This aerial view from the north showed Main Street as it came to a dead end at Fourteenth on the south. Just beyond that was a line of trees along Stillwater Creek. The Payne County courthouse was in the right foreground and the railroad tracks formed a semi-circle at th left of picture. Sixth Street was only two lanes then.
Courtesy Oklahoma State University Library, Special Collections

Can you recognize this familiar scene as it appeared in the early 1930s? The dirt lane is West Sixth from Adams almost to Walnut. George W. Lewis' farm house is still there. The Stillwater Medical Center was built on the right. In the foreground Richard S. Ward and his son, Elvin, are delivering about fifty trucks to the U.S. Government.
Courtesy of Irene Ward Bishop

Oil—Boom and Bust

Visions of sugar plums, mink coats, and Rolls Royces danced in the heads of many area oil explorers when this gusher broke loose on the Cecil Jones farm east of Stillwater in 1935. For several days it produced an average of 1,464 barrels a day. Then it collapsed like a deflated balloon, all production ceased, and dreams turned to reality. Courtesy of Mrs. Cecil (Helen) Jones

Stillwater experienced one real oil boom. The discovery well of the Ramsey field six miles southwest of Stillwater began producing oil on January 1, 1938. The next day, two thousand people came to view the site. Almost overnight, the field produced twenty-one million barrels. Two small communities, Gray City and Paradise, sprung up on the edge of the field. The wells were torn down in 1968 as production diminished.
Standing by a well with his granddaughter, Sheryl, is Cecil Jones, who, with Mid-Continent Oil Company opened the Ramsey field.
Courtesy of Mrs. Cecil (Helen) Jones

Shortly after he arrived in Stillwater in 1890, James Ramsey traded his team, wagon, harness and twenty-five dollars cash to a squatter for the farm that became the Ramsey field. He was fifty at the time. He died in 1933, five years before oil was discovered there. The property was divided among his nine children. With him is his wife, Sarah, at their later home at 914 South West Street.
Courtesy of the Ramsey family

Would the Ramsey field bring an avalanche of people and create new boom towns? O. D. Shelton and R. W. Gray hoped so as they laid out a Gray City townsite on the west side of the section line and set up the above office.
Courtesy of the Stillwater Chamber of Commerce

Not to be outdone, Isom, Little, and Bullard set up a townsite office cater-cornered from the Gray City office and sold lots for the town of Paradise. Their efforts were almost fruitless as oil workers and suppliers tended to commute from nearby established towns.
Courtesy of the Stillwater Chamber of Commerce

This cafe was the principal eating place of Ramsey field workers. It offered a wide assortment of sandwiches, plate lunches, and even steaks. The sign shows Murphy and Kiney as proprietors. It was on the east side of the section line.
Courtesy of the Stillwater Chamber of Commerce

Stillwater's first modern hospital was designed and completed in only thirty days to
qualify for federal aid. Built at 1510 West
Ninth Street, the hospital opened October
29, 1939. Its forty-bed capacity was expanded to eighty-five in 1949-1950. Over the
years, the city leased the hospital to the
Sisters of the Precious Blood, the Baptist
General Convention, National Medical
Centers, Inc., and to General Health
Services. The hospital was closed when a
new medical center opened in 1976. It was
demolished in 1978 and a medical office
complex is now on the site.
Courtesy of the Sheerar Museum,
Jaycee Scrapbook, 1954

*Duck Street was for many years a quiet
tree-lined boulevard, as shown in this view
looking north from the Methodist Church.
Commercial development and the growth of
the university have made it a busy artery.
The median was removed in 1966.
Courtesy of the City of Stillwater*

For more than thirty-five years, Crystal Plunge was Stillwater's favorite swimming hole. Built in 1928, the pool was located in a secluded area south of East Sixth Street in the shadow of the Stillwater Milling Co. The Stark family, first M. L. and later his son and daughter-in-law, Vernon and Esther Stark, operated the pool for years. From 1965 until 1969, the pool was operated by Future Growth, Inc., whose stockholders included many prominent Stillwater Citizens. Crystal Plunge closed after Oklahoma State University, Country Club, and the Elks Club built facilities that included pools. Stillwater's Municipal Pool opened in 1973 to provide new public facilities.
Courtesy of Shideler's Photo Craft

After a bond issue in 1938, a new Stillwater Municipal Building was constructed in 1939 on the corner of Eighth and Lewis streets where the Whittenberg Hospital formerly stood. Before that, city offices were across the street southwest, some of them on the alley just off Lewis. Several additions have been made to the building since 1939.
Courtesy of Mrs. Helen Posey

185

1941—A Historic Year for the Press

A well known figure in Oklahoma and Stillwater newspaper history, Willis F. Allen (pictured here) purchased the weekly Payne County News *in 1929 with Lloyd Evans as a partner. The plant was at 114 West Eighth Street. In 1935, Allen began publishing Tuesday, Thursday, and Sunday issues of the* Stillwater News. *Allen sold his two newspapers in 1940 to E. E. (Hook) Johnson and Irvin Hurst, who in turn sold them in 1941 to Charles Robert Bellatti. Allen had formerly published newspapers at Wagoner, Vinita, Pryor, Hominy, Pawnee, and Duncan.*
Courtesy of Robert L. Evans

The young John Painter Hinkel was a pioneer in Payne County journalism. He and his wife founded the Perkins Journal *in January 1892. In 1904 he purchased the Stillwater* Gazette *from Charles Neerman. Then in 1912 he took over the Stillwater* Press *from George Gelder. Hinkel was the first postmaster at Ripley and the second at Perkins.*
Courtesy of Mary Hinkel Herron

He began his career as an attorney in 1912 at Blackwell, but in 1919, Charles Robert Bellatti decided to become a newspaperman. He purchased the Blackwell Daily Tribune *and built the circulation to fourteen thousand. In 1940, Bellatti sold his interests there and began anew in Stillwater, which he believed would become the best town in central Oklahoma. He combined existing newspapers to create the Daily* News-Press, *and in 1947 established Radio station KSPI. Through his association with state and national leaders, he was instrumental in bringing highways and other civic improvements to Stillwater.*
Courtesy of the NewsPress

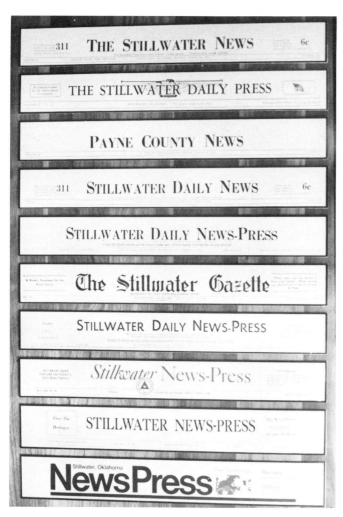

These newspaper "masts" reflect changes in Stillwater newspapers starting in 1941. C. R. (Robert) Bellatti first purchased the Stillwater News and Payne County News from Everett E. Johnson and Irvin Hurst. On November 9, 1941, he purchased the Stillwater Daily Press and the Stillwater Gazette from the John P. Hinkel family. These evolved into the Stillwater Daily News-Press and in 1981 to the present NewsPress mast.
Photo by Scott Carter, the NewsPress

Although Eli Shonbrun testified that Madeline Webb was innocent, she received a life sentence to Westfield, New York State Farm for Women. She became a model prisoner and was paroled in January 1967. She returned to Stillwater and became a leader in community affairs, especially in efforts to preserve Stillwater's heritage.

She compiled a directory of historic homes and started a Heritage Days celebration. Gov. Nelson Rockefeller of New York issued a pardon for Madeline in 1974. She died February 16, 1980, and a Heritage Essay Contest was established in her honor. Madeline loved animals. She is shown here at her home on Hartford Street holding three puppies.
Courtesy of Jonita Milligan

A Country Girl And a City Murder

A sensational murder trial stirred Stillwater toward the end of the Country Years. Madeline Webb, above, Stillwater High school graduate and 1933 Oklahoma Agricultural and Mechanical College beauty queen, was charged along with her lover, Eli Shonbrun, and two others, in the murder of Mrs. Susan Reich, fifty-two, a Polish refugee in New York's Sutton Hotel on March 4, 1942. Mrs. Reich was robbed of two thousand dollars in diamonds. Madeline's mother sent James M. Springer, Sr., on the left, of Stillwater to defend her. New York newspapers portrayed him as "an old frontier lawyer from the cattle town of Stillwater, Oklahoma, who never lost a client to the death penalty." The co-defense attorney on the right, was Jacques Britenkank of New York. Courtesy of James M. Springer, Jr.

187

Chapter 13

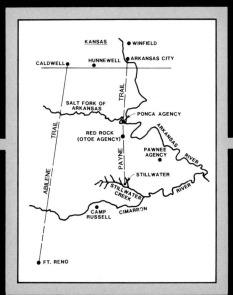

GROWING INTO A CITY

The post-World War II era was one of great awakening for Stillwater. First came the rapid expansion of Oklahoma A & M College as more than five thousand war veterans sent enrollment spiraling to new heights. Then came a move to diversify Stillwater's economy to make it less dependent on the college. In 1951, this brought about the Industrial Foundation, which sought to show Stillwater's advantages as an industrial center. Since its creation, the foundation has changed the face, substance, and economy of Stillwater.

Clee Fitzgerald, attorney and long-time president of the foundation, said as the search for industry began, "I don't know much about industry, I just know that industry makes things out of stuff. And, in the process, this causes the investment of capital, which creates payrolls. This, in general, raises the values of property any place around it." His analysis, although perhaps oversimplified, proved correct.

The new era brought about determined and energetic new leadership to Stillwater. In the beginning, Robert A. Lowry, Amon W. Swope, Orlando M. Eyler, Frank J. Wikoff and a dozen others like them fought for Stillwater's future. Now as the second fifty years of the town began, a new breed was anxious to get moving. The postwar era brought an infusion of talent and ideas such as Stillwater had not known. Some were a part of Oklahoma Agricultural and Mechanical College's great growth and included students and faculty from all parts of the country. The college was beginning to hire fewer of its own graduates, to liberalize its curriculum and to expand graduate work in preparation for its new status as Oklahoma State University.

Others providing new leadership were veterans eager to get back into civilan clothes and build a new life. Among these were sons of pioneer Stillwater business people who came back with their own ideas about making their home town better. In more recent years, women began to play more important roles and to assume leadership in all facets of Stillwater life. The men welcomed them.

Helping make the transition from the old to the new were many established community builders, including Roy T. Hoke, Harley Thomas, C. R. (Robert) Bellatti, Wyche Murphy, Sr., Sam Myers, and Claude Bradshaw. They were among the leaders working for new highways, better streets, and countless other improvements.

The new era changes were phenomenal. Perkins Road, once a dirt lane a fourth of a mile outside the town, is now a major commercial and industrial artery, and the city limits have expanded eastward beyond that to near Brush Creek. Once Western Avenue was a dirt road that bordered the farms of Louis J. Jardot, Frank McFarland, and Simon P. Duck. Now the city limits reach beyond Western and on past Country Club Road.

Vast housing additions sprang up in all directions, but especially to the southwest and northeast. Once, apartments were a part of frame homes near the campus. Now modern brick developments are everywhere. A modern medical center, a new post office, and a new high school were a part of the great change.

Stillwater's growth was not all commercial, industrial, or academic. The new era brought a profound interest in culture. The Arts and Humanities Council, founded in 1968, led the drive for cultural development. One of its projects was the Sheerar Museum. Town and Gown brought university and town people together for theatrical productions. The Payne County Historical Society took on new life as newcomers joined long time residents to preserve Stillwater's heritage.

These were but some of the factors in transforming Stillwater from a country town into a modern small city of forty-two thousand and laying the groundwork for its growth into a medium-sized city of the future.

As soon as the Industrial Foundation was established, Stillwater's business leaders stepped out in style to get results. Ready for an industrial tour in 1952 were, front row: Joe Human, Parker Norton, Warren B. Cooke, G. Wilson Duncan, Roy Bradley, Clark Dunn, Richard Facker, Leroy Crossman, Morris Gershon, and Fritz Weilmuenster; second row: Arlie Tomlinson, unidentified, Bill Abbott, Bink Simank, Glen Varnum, Walter Hoss, Mayor A. B. Alcott, Roy T. Hoke, Jr., and Jay Fennell; back row: Ralph Archer, Karl Friedemann, Bill Noske, Edmund W. (Si) Simank, Glenn Ward, Leonard F. (Mike) Sheerar, Alvin Murphy, Herb Loyd, R. O. Fox, and Tom Bates.
Courtesy of Gerald E. Bradshaw

In 1978, these men were Industrial Foundation trustees working for new industry. Seated are Sam Myers, secretary-treasurer; Clee Fitzgerald, president, and Dr. Richard W. Poole, OSU vice-president and professor of economics. In back are Owen Thomas, Lawrence Gish, Larry Hansen, Sam Carpenter, Jerry Miller, Gerald Bradshaw, and Robert McCormick.
Courtesy of Mrs. Wiliam R. (Mary K.) Wright

*William R. (Bill) Wright was a major factor in bringing industry to Stillwater. Starting in 1959, Wright was for fourteen years simultaneously executive director of the Industrial Foundation and the Stillwater Chamber of Commerce. During this period, Moore Business Forms, Swan Rubber, Mercury Marine, and National Standard all chose Stillwater for plant sites.
Courtesy of Mrs. William R.
(Mary K.) Wright*

*As Stillwater grew into a city and Oklahoma Agricultural and Mechanical College became Oklahoma State University, these men took on the task of coordinating activities that brought about closer ties between the two. Chairman Claude Bradshaw is seated. Standing are (left to right) Lawrence F. (Chub) Bellatti, Bob Fenimore, Vic Thompson, Bill Bernhardt, Roy T. Hoke, Jr., and Sam Bates.
Courtesy of Gerald E. Bradshaw*

**Major Industries Herald
A New Era**

*A new era began in Stillwater with the completion in 1966 of the Moore plant, the first of Stillwater's big industries. From a beginning of 82 employees, the plant's locally based workforce in 1988 had grown to more than 280. The plant's main focus is the manufacture of business forms for data processing, but equally important is the production of Moore Clean Print® carbonless paper, which can be used instead of carbon tissues to make the copies in multiple-part business forms. One of Moore's largest production facilities, the Stillwater plant serves customers throughout the southern and western United States.
Photo by Gary Lawson, the NewsPress*

Mercury Marine made the greatest impact on Stillwater's industrial development on September 21, 1973. The company announced it would build a $28 million, 500,000-square-foot industrial plant employing 500 people on a 232-acre tract at North Perkins and Airport roads. The plant was completed in 1975 and began production of MerCruiser stern drives. It has grown far beyond expectations and in 1988 had 1,350 employees. It was the largest single plant investment in the history of the Brunswick Company of Chicago, Mercury Marine's parent company.
Photo by Gary Lawson, the NewsPress

Stillwater's National-Standard plant (in foreground) was in 1988 the leading domestic producer of tire bead wire and welding wire. It began in August 1974 with a work force of twenty-five. The 50,000-square-foot training facility at 3602 North Perkins Road opened in October. The facilities were expanded in 1975 and 1977 and contained 305,520 square feet. National-Standard was operating plants in six other countries and its products were being exported to more than one hundred countries in all parts of the world. The plant in 1988 had 207 employees and the number has reached as high as 300.
Photo by Gary Lawson, the NewsPress

World Color Press, the world's largest printer of newsstand magazines, opened a Stillwater plant, Oberlin Color Press, on April 12, 1984 at 100 West Airport Road. In 1988, the plant had 200 employees with an annual payroll of approximately five million dollars, but had just completed a five-year agreement with Time, Inc., to print Life Magazine, *which could add another 100 employees. Oberlin prints and binds 1,400,000 copies of* Rolling Stone *every other week, and millions of newspaper advertising inserts.*
Photo by Gary Lawson, the NewsPress

Armstrong World Industries, Inc., arrived in Stillwater early in 1988. After revamping the plant formerly occupied by Swan Rubber at 4115 North Perkins Road and adding a 100,000-square-foot warehouse, the company began production in the summer of 1988 of "wide-width" rotogravure sheet flooring materials. The company planned to have 150 employees by year's end.
Photo by Gary Lawson, the NewsPress

Washinka & Son jewelers welcomed the post-World War II period with a remodeling job that included such novelties as sliding glass doors on display windows, blond furniture, and silverware with four plates of silver. The Washinkas operated at 616 South Main from 1932-1964. Front to back are J. C. Washinka, Mrs. Edna Washinka, Jack Washinka, Mrs. Jack (Marville) Washinka, and Mrs. Lala Bailey, an employee.
Courtesy of Marville Washinka

The postwar changing face of Stillwater is reflected in this picture of the seven hundred block of South Main in the early 1950s. Once the block boasted such names as Van Horn Drugs, McBride's Men's Wear, Smith Studio, Murl Penney's Booterie, Earnest Bros., the Mecca Theatre and Jim Arneson's Parisian store. All are gone now. J.C. Penney Company and Tiger Drug were once in this block but have moved to other locations.
Courtesy of the City of Stillwater

The changing scene in Stillwater after World War II inspired three individuals to consider whether the time had come for some type of community theatre. After informal sessions in the Student Union, John Woodworth, director of campus radio services, James C. Stratton, professor of journalism, and Mrs. Peyton (Marguerite) Glass, Jr., called a meeting in the fall of 1951. Out of this grew Town and Gown, an organization for both town and academic people. The first production came in January 1952 with the staging of Somerset Maugham's The Constant Wife. The cast, pictured are John Woodworth in front; (second row), Eleanor Schlaretzki, Joan Lewis, and Flossie Hough; (third row) Esther Stark and Mona Pierson; (back row) Craig Hampton, Dick Draper, and Ed Burris.
Courtesy of Town and Gown

During the first ten years, Town and Gown presented its plays in the student union ballroom, but in April 1962 it purchased this building on South Boomer Road near the intersection with Perkins Road. The building has been remodeled several times.
Photo by the author

Another sign that Stillwater was becoming "citified" came in 1958 with the beginning of telephone direct dialing. Clarence Cowan, Southwestern Bell manager from 1938 to 1965, holds an old style phone with crank that had been used on his father's farm since 1900. Beside it is the first Stillwater dial phone.
Courtesy of Clarence Cowan

Malinda Diggs Berry brought a major honor to Stillwater in 1959 when she was chosen over nineteen other finalists representing thirteen cotton belt states as America's Maid of Cotton. A beauty queen and honor student at OSU, Malinda became the first Maid of Cotton to travel around the world with stops that included London, Athens, Karachi, Bombay, Tokyo, and Sydney. Her parents were Mr. and Mrs. Thomas E. Berry.
Courtesy of Malinda Berry Fischer

Stillwater and Boomer creeks both ran amuck after 10.95 inches of rain fell between October 1 and 4, 1959, causing the worst flood in Stillwater history. More than 675 families abandoned their homes. Water critically damaged twelve thousand acres of farmland. This aerial view is from the north looking down from McElroy Street to an area between North Main and the railroad tracks. Many flood control measures have been instituted since 1959 to prevent a recurrence.
Courtesy of Mrs. William R.
(Mary K.) Wright

197

Off We Go to the Suburbs

In the 1950s, American families began to move to the suburbs. Stillwater's first major suburban housing development was the Zuck Addition off Nineteenth Street in the southwest. It was first platted as Meadow Park Subdivision. Developers were John B. and Thelma Zuck. Just south of Zuck Addition is Quail Ridge Development, platted October 18, 1965 by Leland Peters and the P. & L. Development Company.
Photo by Gary Lawson, the NewsPress

A memorable fishing and swimming hole of Stillwater youngsters disappeared when Dr. Buel Staton and John Head developed the Sangre Ridge Addition in 1963. The land was formerly known as the Old Leininger Lake property. The section line in the background became Sangre Road. The lake and entrance to Sangre Ridge are at upper left.
Photo by Gary Lawson, the NewsPress

"What we need around here is a new private course," William A. Andrews said to his golf partner, Dr. Powell E. Fry, after the two waited in a long line at a municipal golf course in 1964. The two talked, dreamed, and then planned. Out of this grew the Stillwater Golf and Country Club Addition. Twenty-four investors put up four thousand dollars each to buy the former Lake Park Country Club. On March 21, 1966, the new addition was platted. This view is form the south. Photo by Gary Lawson, the NewsPress

The first major housing additions for middle and upper middle income families were all in the southwest, but in 1973, the Park View Estates offered an alternative in the northeast. Developed by Mr. and Mrs. J. C. Rogers, the addition covers one hun- *dred sixty acres bordering on North Perkins and Richmond roads. It was designed by Phillips and Stong Engineering Company. The land was originally homesteaded by the Chris A. Holzer family in 1889. Photo by Gary Lawson, the* NewsPress

When Stillwater's population reached twenty-five thousand in 1960, it meant that South High and Junior High could no longer accommodate the growing school population. This brought about construction of the new C. E. Donart High School on a thirty-one-acre tract on North Boomer Road. It included sixty classrooms and cost $904,508. Several additions have been made since it was built.
Courtesy of the Stillwater Chamber of Commerce

When the new high school opened in 1960, it was named C. E. Donart School to honor the man who had given a half-century of service as clerk of the Board of Education. Charles E. ("Elmer") Donart became clerk in 1911 and remained in office until 1962. He was also president of the First National Bank from 1929-1957. He was a brother of Harry Donart, who taught in Stillwater's first school.
Courtesy of Barbara Hartley Dunn and Mrs. C. E. (Ruth) Donart

The Indian Meridian Area Vocational-Technical School that opened on August 25, 1975, added a new dimension to Stillwater as an educational and training center. The project began in 1972 when school districts of Glencoe, Guthrie, Morrison, Mulhall-Orlando, Pawnee, and Stillwater decided they should have their own technical school. On June 19, 1973, voters approved a $1.7 million bond issue. The new school was built on a forty-acre tract just off Sangre Road on the southwest edge of Stillwater. Ben Wesley, an eleven year old from Mulhall, provided the name in a contest. Photo by Gary Lawson, the NewsPress

"'If Everyone Rides, Who'll Pull the Wagon?'"

Charles W. ("Bill") Thomas's record of community service may be unparalleled in Stillwater history. In 1966, city leaders compiled a book of his achievements and ended with six volumes. His favorite saying was "If everyone rides, who'll pull the wagon?" More often than not it was Thomas who did the pulling—for civil defense, airport, YMCA, county fair, schools, Boy Scouts, industrial development, Red Cross, Stillwater Medical Center, United Fund and countless other projects. He was mayor from 1972 to 1976 and again from 1979 to 1982. His greatest achievement was his leadership to secure the Kaw Water project. He was president of many organizations, including the Rotary Club and the Chamber of Commerce.

An impatient, restless man, Thomas has not been popular with everyone. He was defeated for re-election after the success of the Kaw Water Project, largely because he was inclined to push people who were standing still while he wanted to get moving. He has been honored many times. He was most proud of the Saturday Evening Post *Award in 1967 as National Automobile Dealer of the Year. On April 21, 1976, state and city leaders paid tribute to Thomas when Acting Governor George Nigh proclaimed it "Bill Thomas Day in Oklahoma."*

Born September 20, 1921, Thomas is a 1939 graduate of Stillwater High School. He earned a bachelor of science degree from OSU in 1947. He was manager of the Stillwater Ford agency for his father, Hurley, from 1947 to 1950, and a co-owner from 1950 to 1976 when he sold his interest to his brother Owen.

Courtesy of the NewsPress

Gov. Henry Bellmon in April 1966 selected the Thomas family as the number one physical fitness family of the year in Oklahoma. Here, Bill and Virginia have fun with their children on a snowy day. In the front row are Susie and Carolyn; center row, Harley and Betty. Mrs. Thomas's civic contributions rival those of her husband. She has been a leader in the Arts and Humanities Council, Stillwater Junior Service League Sustainers, Girl Scouts, Boy Scouts (son Harley is an Eagle Scout), civil defense, United Way, and Payne County Historical Society. She has been president of PEO Club, the Parent Teachers Association Council, and Rotary Anns. She was for five years chairwoman of the American Legion Auxiliary Girls State.
Courtesy of C. W. ("Bill") Thomas

A new era in health care for north central Oklahoma began on January 10, 1976 with the opening of the Stillwater Medical Center (SMC). The new facility attracted physicians of many specialties. Donations from the community enabled SMC to be among the first to add laser surgery equipment and the CAT scan. The additions quickly made SMC a regional referral center with forty percent of its patients coming from the surrounding area. It is now recognized as the leading health care center in north central Oklahoma. This rare photo shows the old Municipal Hospital in the background. Courtesy of Gerald E. Bradshaw.

Sam Bates (seated), chairman of the Stillwater Medical Center Board of Trustees for twelve years, stepped down in 1988. Next to Bates is Mrs. William R. (Mary) Wright, SMC auxiliary supervisor and for twelve years secretary to hospital administrator Robert E. Park. Standing left to right are Eric Williams, D.V.M., who succeeded Bates; Lynn R. Osborn, attorney; and Tom Covington, M.D.

Of Bates, Park said, "He has devoted thousands of hours to provide health care for Stillwater people. His maturity and thoughtful leadership have kept our hospital from facing the political and financial problems of most hospitals. He has been so instrumental in our getting new equipment and facilities. He is fair, committed, and complete in his investigations and actions. He and other board members are all volunteers." Courtesy of the Stillwater Medical Center

203

If Stillwater were to choose a "Citizen of the Century," it might well be Roy T. Hoke, who was known for his civic contributions and philanthropies from the early days through its years as a city. Although he never sought major public office, he was a powerful figure working quietly for civic improvements and better highways. His major concern was public health and he served on the Payne County Medical Board for more than fifty years. He gave generously to health causes, especially at Stillwater Medical Center, and also to projects involving public schools, universities, and churches.

Hoke was a charter member of the Stillwater Lions Club and its first president. In 1985, he was honored for sixty-three years of perfect attendance. In 1984, he was inducted into the Oklahoma State University Alumni Hall of Fame. He received many other citations, among them one from the Exchange Club that described him as a "mover, motivator, leader, humanitarian, builder, unselfish, and humble servant."

Born at Quay, near Yale, October 31, 1895, he came to Stillwater in 1917 to attend Oklahoma Agricultrual and Mechanical College prep school. In 1919 he purchased a building at 125 West Seventh, enlarged it, and named it the Hoke Building. It is now on the state's register of historic buildings. Although he was engaged in real estate and other enterprises, he was best known for the Roy T. Hoke Lumber Company. He died September 1, 1987, at age ninety-one.
Courtesy of Helt Studio

The Kaw Water Treatment Plant north of Stillwater just off Highway 177 may assure the city of an adequate water supply until 2075. It began with a twelve million dollar bond issue in 1979 that passed by only forty-six votes. In late 1981, a pipeline from the Kaw Reservoir near Ponca City was completed and plant construction began. On January 10, 1986, the plant was dedicated to Bill Thomas at a ceremony marking its completion.
Photo by the author

A new era in Stillwater also brought a new post office in 1980. The facility moved from Husband Street to the eight hundred block of Lewis, making it the ninth post office location since 1889. The Linden Hotel and Dr. W. C. Whittenberg's first hospital were previously on the site.
Photo by the author

Christine F. Salmon made history in 1982
when she became Stillwater's first woman
mayor, defeating incumbent Bill Thomas.
An architect by profession, she was professor
of housing and interior design at OSU for
twenty years. In 1982, she was named to the
Oklahoma Women's Hall of Fame. She died
October 10, 1985 after a twenty-five year
battle against cancer. Ninth and Main
Plaza was renamed Christine F. Salmon
Plaza as a tribute to her service as "mayor,
humanitarian, and tireless civic worker,
and for her outstanding contributions to
the city of Stillwater."
Courtesy of the NewsPress

It was an old building but a giant step forward in 1958 when Stillwater's first family YMCA began operations in this house at 204 South Duck. Workmen are shown getting it in shape. The new "Y" represented a merger of the city's and OSU's YMCAs and the YWCA. The first YMCA in Stillwater was organized when Dr. Angelo C. Scott, OAMC president, called a meeting at the Methodist Church on March 22, 1900. Courtesy of the YMCA

An average of sixteen thousand citizens a year participate in family YMCA activities since the modern facility above replaced the original structure at 204 South Duck. The first phase of the new building was dedicated in 1968 and the second phase was completed in 1980. Age groups from preschool to senior citizens participate in activities that include physical fitness classes, handball, swimming, and basketball. Photo by the author

Chapter 14

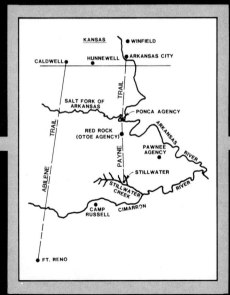

THE COUNTRY SPIRIT SURVIVES

At times it seems country life has disappeared from Stillwater. The industrial development along Perkins Road, heavy traffic, and busy shopping centers suggest that commercial growth and the university are the only centers of activity. Certainly, farmers and cattlemen who once clustered on Stillwater street corners giving it a casual, friendly appearance, are much less visible.

These signs are misleading. Agriculture, like other facets of life, has changed, but it is very much alive and important to the community. As the county seat, Stillwater serves as the agricultural center for Payne County, and because of Oklahoma State University, it is still to many the agricultural capital of Oklahoma.

Family firms still operate throughout the county. Duane McVey, county extension agricultural agent and extension director, estimates the total monetary value of crops, cattle, and dairy products is approximately twenty million dollars a year. About ten million dollars of this is from beef cattle production. Payne County at this writing has thirty-nine Grade-A dairies whose annual production is between four-and-a-half and five million dollars.

High-tech has come to the farm and at least six dairies are computerized. The computer, among other things, determines when and how much to feed the calves. The stereotype of the typical farm home, stemming from depression days, was a frame house with outside privy and a water well. Today the typical farmer or cattleman may be living in a well-landscaped modern brick home. He still comes to town but his attire may be sports clothes or even a tie rather than overalls or denim. He probably is better educated and more sophisticated than his predecessors.

The best way to understand the scope of agriculture in Stillwater is to visit the Payne County Fair or other major events held at the fairgrounds east of town. More than 20,000 people came to the 1987 fair to view 3,269 exhibits of all kinds. The fair facility consists of six buildings, two of which have air conditioning and heating. The arena building is 26,400 square feet. Three livestock barns bring the total of the complex to 68,400 square feet.

In addition to the fair, more than sixty-five other events are scheduled during the year that bring agricultural people together. These include the Sooner State Dairy Show, the Cheese and Sausage Festival, the Northeast Angus Sale, and the Oklahoma State Breeders Association Tested Boar Sale.

Payne County also has extensive programs in soil and water conservation. Much of this began on May 14, 1941 when the Payne County Conservation District was organized. Of the county's 448,000 acres, 93,000 acres are considered cropland with wheat and alfalfa the principal crops. About 277,000 acres are in pastureland or native rangeland. Conservation practices in use include terraces, erosion control structures, ponds, and weed control.

Larry Poindexter, district conservationist of the USDA Soil Conservation Service, says Payne County also has an active flood prevention program. Underway at this writing are three small watershed projects which involve dams to retain flood water and some channel improvements. The latter are on Long Branch, Lower Black Bear, and Stillwater creeks. Poindexter says the projects will be major factors in reducing flooding problems in the county.

Agriculture is a center of activity and interest for young people, too. More than one thousand youths in Stillwater and Payne County belong to 4-H clubs and the Future Farmers of America. One major youth activity is the Payne county Junior Livestock Show each September.

*George Knotts lived in a dugout on the
banks of Stillwater Creek west of town after
the 1889 Land Run. Every time it rained,
his dugout was flooded. Disgusted, he
moved first south of town and then to Yost
Lake Road where he operated the first
jackass ranch in the area.
Courtesy of Marie Sherrill Rainwater*

William W. Abercrombie, a veteran of ten major Civil War battles, established this cotton gin on East Sixth in 1900 with his son-in-law, Peter D. Miller, as partner. In 1896, the two started a gin and a small electric power plant on Lewis Street, but as the railroad arrived, they moved it to East Sixth. There they built a larger power plant that for a time provided electrical power for the city.
Courtesy of the Archives and Manuscripts Division, Oklahoma Historical Society

The Farmers Co-op owned this cotton gin started in about 1907 on Twelfth Street and Perkins Road. When it was destroyed in the early 1920s by fire, the Stillwater Cotton and Grain Company bought the property. The billboard at left advertises Katz Bros. dry goods store.
Courtesy of Mrs. Fay Hull

From 1929 to 1957, the Stillwater Cotton and Grain Company operated this cotton gin on Twelfth and Perkins Road after taking over from the Farmers Co-op. Elijah Cook of Guthrie was president, A. H. Rickstrew of Meridian was vice-president, and Carol Rickstrew of Stillwater was secretary-treasurer. The company also sold coal, feed, and farm machinery.
Courtesy of the Western History Collections, University of Oklahoma

Cotton was king in Payne County in the early years, and farmers stood in line at the gins. Carol Rickstrew, an operator of the Stillwater Cotton and Grain Company for twenty-nine years, estimated that from two to three thousand bales of cotton a year were ginned in Stillwater alone. Cotton farming declined when it became difficult to find workers to do the chopping and pick the cotton. As automation took over the chores, most farmers found their equipment more adaptable to small grains.
Courtesy of the Western History Collections University of Oklahoma

From 1915 to 1923, most Payne County farmers could not afford the high-tech equipment shown in this photo. They cut, shocked, and cured the wheat or oats, then threshing crews traveled over the county to finish the job. Oliver D. Kinzie, whose father homesteaded a farm west of Cushing in 1891, and his brother, Charley, who owned a farm south of Stillwater, made the rounds in Payne County in the early 1920s. The pulley from the ancient steamer was operating the thresher on the right.
Courtesy of Oliver H. Kinzie

Neighbors joined in to form a harvesting crew. Here a team of horses pulls a wagon load of grain to the thresher as Oliver D. Kinzie supervises the operation. Wagons went through the field and "pitchers" tossed bundles of wheat into them. After the day's work, the harvest hands ate dinner at the farm house where the threshing was being done.
Courtesy of Oliver H. Kinzie

A favorite shopping place of farmers was Greiner Bros. store at Ninth and Main streets. A specialty there was knee pads made from tires for cotton pickers. The brothers, Alphonse and Pious, disliked their names intensely and were known as "A.M." and "P.M." A.M. made the 1889 run into Perry. They handled Banner buggies and surreys. Horse collars hang from the store ceiling and walls. A wide assortment of horse blankets is on the counter. A.M. is in foreground and his brother in background.
Courtesy of Lawrence Gibbs

The equal rights for women campaign of the 1980s may have had a forerunner in this meeting in June 1924 when Stillwater farm women began a "Swat the Rooster" campaign. They urged everyone to kill, sell, or pen all their roosters, which apparently were making themselves obnoxious to the hens.
Courtesy of Duane McVey,
Payne County Extension Director

The towering Stillwater Milling Company has long been a symbol of Stillwater's importance as an agricultural center. The mill closed out its flour-making operations in 1956 and now manufactures formula feeds for use in production of meat, milk, and eggs. The elevator was built in 1957. In 1988, the mill had ninety employees and a sales volume of about sixty million dollars a year. Its sales totaled about three million bushels of wheat a year in domestic and export markets. The mill has been a major factor in bringing and maintaining rail service to Stillwater.
Photo by the author

The Stillwater mill in 1924 was next to B. A. Ray's cotton gin on the south side of East Sixth Street. The establishment was destroyed by fire so many times before 1900 that people became superstitious and were afraid to work there. The central part of the mill is still there, a part of today's much larger structure.
Courtesy of the City of Stillwater

Landowners around Stillwater and through-
out the county have installed thousands of
ponds such as this one on Dr. O. M.
Rippey's farm. The ponds have helped
control erosion, provide livestock water,
and improve fish and wildlife habitats.
Photo by Paul Newlin, the NewsPress

**The Payne County Fair—
Going Strong Since 1890**

*Payne County Fairgrounds shown here
were busy in the early 1930s when they*
*was a major activity. Some horse-drawn
racing vehicles used wheels from cultivators.
The grounds moved to the Couch Park area
in about 1915 and then to the present
location east of Stillwater in 1971.*
*moved to the Couch Park area in about
1915 and then to the present location east of
Stillwater in 1971.
Courtesy of the Oklahoma State University
Library, Special Collections*

*The Oklahoma Junior Beef Expo was in
progress when this aerial photo of the present Payne County Fairgrounds on Highway 51 East was taken in June 1988. This
view is from the south. The large center*
*building is the show arena. To its left are
exhibit and community buildings. Livestock
barns are on the right. The complex opened
in 1971, and covers 68,400 feet.
Photo by Gary Lawson, the NewsPress*

Between judging and contests, the rural people of Payne County, and even some city folks, enjoyed the carnival midway of the fair. More than twenty thousand attended in 1987.
Photo by Paul Newlin, the NewsPress

"Soo-e-e-e pig!" the crowds yelled at the fair's annual pig race. The animals had coaching and training ahead of time. The pigs lived up to their reputation as they sped around the track, knowing that feed was at the end. Their favorite delicacy was cookies.
Photo by Paul Newlin, the NewsPress

The 4-H club booth at the Payne County fair in 1987 was a favorite congregating place for young people. The county had eleven clubs with membership totaling more than five hundred. Among twelve major annual 4-H events were the Junior Livestock Show, Junior Round-Up, and a 4-H Dress Revue and Appropriate Dress Contest.
Photo by Paul Newlin, the NewsPress

Chapter 15

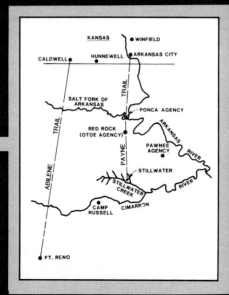

REMINDERS OF THE PAST

As the tide of progress changed Stillwater after World War II, it obliterated treasured relics of the past. All downtown theatres are gone, including the Opera House, the Camera, the Alamo, and in later years, the Aggie and the Leachman. All hotels have disappeared from the original townsite, including the Youst, Going, Linden, Grand, and Rains. Stores occupied by pioneer merchants have given way to new establishments or are covered with modern fronts. Pictures in other chapters show many of these structures as they were in early days.

Homes have changed, too. Once the fashionable homes were on Duck, Lewis, Husband, Main, and other streets close to town or the university. Many of these have yielded to commercial development. Others were replaced by newer homes in the 1920s and 1930s.

Yet, reminders of Stillwater's exciting past are visible in and around the city. On the southern outskirts is the concrete base of a town water well, the last remnant of Payne Center, Stillwater's rival for the county seat. This is just off South Husband Street south of Forty-seventh.

On East Nineteenth Street at Boomer Creek is a marker denoting the site of William L. Couch's 1884 Boomer colony. The exact location of the site is uncertain but was near where Stillwater Creek and Boomer Creek converge. John H. Barnes found ruins of Boomer cabins as far west as the former Charles C. Platt home at 1304 South Main Street.

Sixteen miles east of Stillwater on old Highway 51 is a monument the Payne Historical Society has erected to commemorate the Civil War Battle of Round Mountain site, and on the northern edge of town on Highway 177 between Cherokee and Ranch streets is a historical marker on the line from which the founding fathers made the 1889 Land Run into Stillwater and from which thousands of others rushed into the Cherokee Strip in 1893. This is now the city limits.

Many remnants of the past are in the central part of Stillwater. Orlando M. Eyler's house built in 1893 at 1109 South Main Street still stands. Near there at 215 East Twelfth Street is the Stillwater school service building, the center of which is the original Lincoln School built in 1898.

Once, Ninth and Main was the center of town and the dividing line for street numbers. Will and Ambrose Swiler established the first retail store at 908 South Main. The

original store is gone but the building in which they operated into the 1930s is still there. Across the street is the Lytton building, built in 1901 by Dale Lytton, a founder of the First Christian Church and an early day mayor.

Around the corner in the one hundred block of East Ninth is the oldest building in Stillwater, a stone structure that housed the Citizens Bank. It appears very much as it did when built in 1894. Across the street from it at 116 East Ninth is the site of the Opera House built by Louis J. Jardot in 1900. The building has been remodeled and modernized several times and bears no resemblance to the original structure, but a small part of the Opera House has been preserved. The globes atop the original building (see page number 83) are now mounted on fence posts in the yard of Jardot's son, Harold, at 2104 East Sixth Street.

One of the Opera House treasures was destroyed in the 1940s. From 1900 until 1920, famous performers signed their names on a dressing room wall beneath the stage. The walls were covered with autographs of famous personalities. They were destroyed during remodeling.

Many other historic reminders exist, including the base of the first water tower on Lewis Street, the first sidewalk and the first brick street surface in the two hundred block of East Ninth, and the former Santa Fe Depot a block further east on Ninth. In the oldest section of Fairlawn Cemetery are markers with names of most of the pioneers who founded and built the early town.

Those who enjoy studying Stillwater's heritage will be surprised at the number of historic homes still in existence. A study by Madeline Webb in 1970 relates the history of more than a score of these. Another by Mary Johnstone Chapel was done as a thesis at Oklahoma State University in 1970. It deals largely with the Orlando M. Eyler home but also lists more than seventy others important to Stillwater's heritage.

A far more vast and comprehensive study was underway in 1988 by Carol Bormann, interior designer in Architectural Services at Oklahoma State University and active member of the Payne County Historical Society. From a study of county tax records, she has compiled a list of more than four hundred homes built in Stillwater from 1889 to 1907 and photographed them.

One phase of her study will be to document the architectural identity of pre-statehood houses. A second phase will be to compile the histories of as many of the houses as possible. Her project will add a new dimension to Stillwater history when it is presented in book form.

A repository for artifacts and displays of Stillwater's culture and heritage is the Sheerar Cultural and Heritage Center on the southwest corner of Seventh and Duncan streets. Named for Mr. and Mrs. Leonard F. Sheerar (Mike and Molly), who donated twenty-five thousand dollars toward the purchase of the building from the First Church of Christ Scientist, the museum opened on May 7, 1973. The Stillwater Arts and Humanities Council originated the idea for the center and conducted a fund drive to match the Sheerar contribution.
Photo by Scott Carter, the NewsPress

Mike and Molly Sheerar stand before a historic button display they presented to the museum. Their twenty-five thousand dollar contribution inspired the drive to purchase the museum building. The Sheerars are known for their aid to humanitarian causes, including a grant that made possible the first YMCA swimming pool in 1962.
Courtesy of the NewsPress

Originally the Citizens Bank built in 1894, this building at 107 East Ninth is now a historic landmark owned by the city. A plaque on the front states it is the oldest building in Stillwater. Amon W. Swope, founder of the first bank at Ninth and Main in 1889, was also a founder of the Citizens Bank.
Courtesy of the NewsPress

Joshua B. Brock, front row center, built the Citizens Bank of 1894. He made the 1889 Land Run, settling southeast of Stillwater. He specialized in stone masonry. Two of his crew members are holding hods, used then to carry concrete, including up ladders. Brock was known for his tobacco-chewing horse. Often he bit off a chew of tobacco and then broke off another for his horse. They both chewed as they looked over the job. Brock's descendants still live on the homestead.
Courtesy of Kirby Brock

The post office was located in this building on the northeast corner of Seventh and Main for at least ten years. It was there in 1906 but had been moved back to the nine hundred block of South Main at the time of this picture of a patriotic rally in 1917. The front of the building has been made square since then. M.G. Searcy's Grocery succeeded the post office in the building. In 1933, Glen Varnum, high school music director, began operating the Chenoweth and Green Music Store there. His family still owns the firm.
Courtesy of the Oklahoma State University Library, Special Collections

This building at 614 South Main Street still stands, although it has changed considerably since the early days. Irving Owen Diggs (on the left) started the Daily Democrat before 1900. Eventually it merged with the Advance and was published by G. R. Gould, father of Chester Gould, creator of the Dick Tracy comic strip. Digg's wife, Malinda Blanche Wise Diggs (not shown), was his partner and a founder of the first Stillwater public library. The Diggs' daughter was Cynthalice Diggs Berry. Their grandchildren are Tom D. Berry and Malinda Berry Fischer.
Courtesy of the Sheerar Museum, Jaycee Scrapbook, 1954

225

From shortly after the townsite was established in 1889 until 1926, Lon and Louis Myers operated a livery barn at 113 East Ninth. Then Louis J. Jardot, his son Harold, and a crew of a half dozen others,

tore down the barn and built the Hull Motor Company. Clarency E. Hull, the owner, had been a partner in one of the first undertaking parlors, and a Hupmobile dealer. His sons, Ray and Ned, operated the

Dodge agency at this location for many years after their father's death. Courtesy of Mrs. Fay Hull

The view of Seventh and Husband streets was snapped from the courthouse in about 1922. It shows the Walker, Selph, and Hoke buildings, built in 1913-1914, all of which are on the National Register of

Historic Places. The buildings were restored in 1983 by Winfrey and Barbara Houston and converted into an office building. The buildings were named for N. F. Walker, Dr. D. H. Selph, and Roy T. Hoke.

In the background are the water tower and the fly-loft of the Opera House where heavy stage props were lifted. Courtesy of the Archives and Manuscripts Division, Oklahoma Historical Society

The southwest corner of Tenth and Main has been a historic hotel site in Stillwater since shortly after the land rush. Hamilton Hueston opened the Hueston Hotel there in the 1890s. The Nichols family took over in the early 1900s and Frank Nichols made the hotel widely known as the "Heinz 57 Hotel" because every table in the restaurant was loaded with Heinz products. A wooden awning that extended then across the front and north side was wide enough for wagons to drive through and unload passengers.

Elvin and Earl Rains purchased the hotel after World War II and for years they maintained the colonial style, dormers, and awning of the Hueston and the Nichols as shown in this 1957 picture. The building has been remodeled since then and has been a restaurant site for several years.
Courtesy of the Stillwater Fire Department

On April 17, 1966, state leaders, historians, and fifteen hundred citizens gathered ten miles west of Stillwater on Highway 51 to dedicate this marker denoting the point of the Indian Meridian. The Meridian, established in 1870, extends from Kansas to the Red River and is the dividing line for ranges east and west in property descriptions. Dr. B. B. Chapman, pictured here, president of the Payne County Historical Society for nineteen years and Oklahoma State University professor, presided at the dedication.
Courtesy of Dr. B. B. Chapman

Homes of Pioneers—
Monuments to the Past

One of Stillwater's most elegant early-day homes was still standing at 623 South Lewis in 1988. William W. Abercrombie, co-owner of one of the first cotton gins, built the home in about 1890. He grew a dense grape arbor in the back that provided shelter to and from the outside privy for his wife and five children. In the kitchen was an ultra-modern convenience: a "pitcher pump" that provided inside well water. Courtesy of Art Daugherty, Jr.

Harry B. Bullen had wed just before coming to Stillwater and he wanted a respectable home for his wife. In early 1890 he built this one at 1001 South Lewis, the first home in the new town with plastered walls. It apparently was well built and maintained for it appeared in 1988 much as it did when occupied April 5, 1890. Photo by the author

After he built the first home at Tenth and Lewis, Harry B. Bullen built two others, one at 318 South West and this one at 504 West Fourth. The Bullen home was a social center where friends gathered for bridge parties, recitals, book reviews, and church meetings. It was in 1988 owned by St. Andrews Episcopal Church, which operated a Thrift Shop there.
Photo by the author

Harold T. Jardot is shown on the southwest corner of Ninth and Lowry streets in front of the historic home built by his father, Louis J. Jardot, in 1905. Still in front of the house in 1988 was the first sidewalk built in Stillwater. This was also the first street covered with brick in 1911 and 1912 after the Santa Fe Railroad agreed to built a new depot if the city would improve the access street and sidewalk. His father built the sidewalk, using six-sided ornamental concrete bricks he made for the project.
Courtesy of Harold T. Jardot

A grove of pecan trees has for years attracted passers-by along Twelfth Street at Adams. William Henry Harrison Adams homesteaded the property in 1889 and his descendants still own it. William's son, Walter, planted more than thirty acres of pecan and walnut trees there from 1929 to 1933. The original Adams home was on a lane leading south to near Stillwater Creek west of the trees. James Homer and Arthur Wesley Adams, two of Oklahoma Agricultural and Mechanical College's first students, lived there.
Photo by the author

Hays Hamilton, who came to Stillwater in 1889, settled on this property which is now 1509 West Ninth. He operated a forty-acre grape vineyard and made wine until 1907. His first house was burned by prohibitionists. His second, pictured here, still stands and was in 1988 occupied by his grandchildren, Hays and Margaret Cross.

Hamilton worked in the Osage Nation as a youth in 1882. He first saw the Stillwater Valley in 1884 when he came to see Couch's Boomer camp. He arrived just after Couch was driven out and the burned cabins were still smoldering.
Photo by the author

Now a volunteer center for Oklahoma State University, this home at West Sixth and Adams streets was built about 1919 by George W. Lewis, who made the Land Run of 1889. Lewis's farm extended from Washington Street to Orchard Lane along Sixth. Even into the 1930s his crops covered the west side of Washington. Lewis also, in April 1889, purchased a part of John H. Barnes's land and the street bordering it was named Lewis.
Photo by the author

In 1903, after operating a feed store in Stillwater since 1896, William A. Frick built this rather ornate and distinctive home at 1016 South West, which was then considered one of Stillwater's prestigious neighborhoods. Unlike many early-day homes, the Frick Victorian style structure *looks much as it did at the turn of the century, although two extra bedrooms, another living room area and bath were added in 1958. The house is on the National Register of Historic Sites.*
Photo by the author

Mrs. Fay L. Hull's home at 910 East Connell is on land originally homesteaded by Oscar M. Morse in 1889. A part of his land was used to establish a site for Oklahoma A&M College. Mr. and Mrs. Joseph Wadley built three rooms there in 1900 and added other rooms and a second story in 1904. The house has been remodeled several times since then. Some of the trees in the yard are nearly one hundred years old. Photo by the author

Asa Lovell stands in front of the house at 1001 South West which the family has owned for sixty years. Lovell was born on a farm near Stillwater and moved to town in 1903. The family built this house in 1907. Asa and his brothers, Arthur and Everett, were known for years as "the oil boys." They operated a retail and wholesale oil business from 1909 until 1975. Asa died September 1, 1987. Photo by the author

This house still stands at 1304 South Main since the early days when Charles C. and Anna Platt, their fourteen children, and Nellie the Shetland pony all called the place home. The house, built in about 1906, is on the land originally homesteaded by John H. Barnes in the area where he found remnants of Boomer cabins. Nellie, near the front door, was brought home as a family pet in the back seat of the 1915 Ford sedan. She roamed the house at will, making her way up and down the stairs with ease. Courtesy of Charles E. and Donna Mae Platt

Peter D. Miller came to Stillwater in 1889 or 1890 and shortly after that built this home on the northwest corner of Fifth and Duncan. Miller and his father-in-law, William W. Abercrombie, first operated a meat market on Main Street and then a cotton gin and small power plant on South Lewis. In 1900 they built another gin and larger power plant on East Sixth.
Photo by the author

Was Dick Tracy, the comic strip detective, born in this house at 409 South Lewis? His creator, Chester Gould, lived here as he began his career in 1919. A native of Pawnee, Chester moved to Stillwater after he finished high school. His father, G. R. Gould, became publisher of the Payne County Advance-Democrat and was later associated with the Oklahoma Agricultural and Mechanical College printing department. After two years at the college, Chester completed his work at Northwestern University in 1923.
Photo by the author

233

Chapter 16

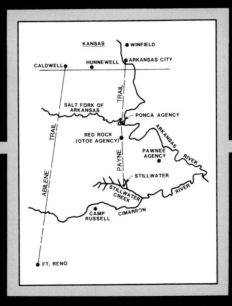

PLANS AND DREAMS FOR 2010

What would the Stillwater pioneers of 1889 say if they could look upon their creation now and observe how succeeding generations have carried on their dream? They would see a small modern city of forty-two thousand with most of the advantages of a metropolitan area but which still retains a country and western flavor. They would see their village has grown into a center of agriculture, engineering, education, culture, and medicine that attracts people from all parts of the world. The pioneers would most likely feel their dream had been realized and would be pleased that neither they nor the monuments they built had been forgotten.

In view of the first century of achievement, one might ask whether the people of Stillwater should pause and enjoy the benefits of the labors of preceding generations. Such is not the case. At this writing, groups of citizens and individuals are busy in all facets of Stillwater life looking to the next one hundred years. Some have plans already on the drawing board. Others have dreams they hope will take shape in the future. The city has developed a comprehensive plan for the year 2010, and Oklahoma State University in 1982 adopted a long-range plan of development concepts. The two entities are working closely together. A few of the projections in the city's comprehensive plan will give at least a glimpse of what Stillwater citizens and their descendants may see in the years ahead.

The city's population in the year 2020 is expected to reach 59,000, and by 2030 it could be 77,000. This will mean residential expansion, and the city estimates there will be 23,814 housing units by 2000. Most of the home building is likely to be in the northeast area convenient to industrial plants. The latter will continue to increase, too, with more plants similar to Mercury Marine, National Standard, Armstrong World Industries, Inc., and World Color Press.

A system of traffic loops around the city is also in the plan for the future. The commuter of 2010 may see an outer loop for a truck route involving Country Club Road, Thirty-second Avenue, Richmond Road, and Fairgrounds Road. A middle loop in the plans would involve Western, Lakeview, and Jardot roads, and Nineteenth Avenue. The third loop would facilitate traffic movement close in and would involve Western, Twelfth, Hall of Fame, Burdick, McElroy and Jardot. Computerizing of traffic signals has already begun and will extend to key intersections in the city.

Beautifying gateways to the city and to Oklahoma State University will be among priorities of the Stillwater Parks and Recreation Department. Director William G. Nelson said the city is especially interested in the historic area north of Sixth Street between the twin bridges near the Stillwater Milling Company. Near there was the first power plant, Morningside Park, and the early city water supply. Murals painted on bricks depicting Stillwater history and a water fountain are under consideration for the site.

Other park areas due for special attention are just west of West Sixth and Washington streets and at the junction of North Washington and Boomer Road.

New landscaping is also on the drawing board for the Boomer Lake area. The lake will be dry for several years while a new dam and road are built across it. When it re-opens, Nelson said, it will have not only new landscaping but additional recreational facilities, including boat rentals, and a jogging trail will surround the lake.

Among the important dreams of citizens and city leaders for the future is a new public library. The city commission, the public library board, and several consulting firms have agreed that Stillwater has outgrown its present library built in 1938. In the future will be a building of approximately twenty-eight thousand square feet. Finding a suitable and available location has been a problem, but citizens seem to prefer a site near the central business district.

Medical Facilities

The Stillwater Medical Center has already had profound impact on medical care in central Oklahoma and those who direct its destiny have important ideas for the future. Among these are an oncology center for treatment of most types of cancer. Phase II providing chemical treatment will begin in 1989.

In 1987, Stillwater citizens expressed great interest in a phobia center and this, too is a dream of the future. A cardiology center and facilities for more out-patient surgery are among other goals. With these may be a continued influx of medical specialists and more medical office buildings south of Stillwater Medical Center.

The plans of today may materialize even before 2010, but what Stillwater will be one hundred years from now may be beyond the imagination. The pioneers dreamed of better wagon trails to make Stillwater a trade center. They were confident of a future water supply when they dug a well on Ninth Street and found water fifty feet down, after Stillwater Creek had become polluted by cows that stood in the stream most of the day.

In 2089, the citizens may look back to 1989. What they will see may appear as primitive to them as the wagon trails seem to this generation. The pioneers could not foresee airplanes, television, space flights, computers, lasers, or nuclear power. Even indoor plumbing was beyond the dreams of most. What this generation considers so modern may be made almost as obsolete in the next century by profound technological advances.

One thing is fairly certain. In the year 2088, citizens will seek a writer or historian to gather the memories, history, and pictures of Stillwater's second 100 years. A book will be needed for the bicentennial celebration. From these will be recorded the story going all the way back to 1989. And what a story it will be. As Eliza Doolittle said to Henry Higgins, "Just you wait." And you'll see!

The view looking north from West Sixth and South Washington streets toward the strip will be considerably different someday. This artist's concept shows one idea OSU has in mind. The plan to improve campus approaches also includes extending University Avenue in a sweeping curve to *South Duck, with attractive landscaping along the way.*
Drawing from "Oklahoma State University, Stillwater Campus Developments Concepts," Sparks, Martin, Easterling/ William Kessler Associates

The Boomer Lake Dam, the narrow road that stretches across it, and the one-lane bridge on the west end are all marked for extinction. A new dam and a road north of the dam are in the future.
Photo by the author

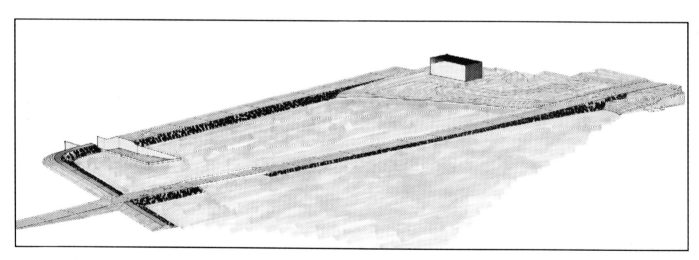

When the new Boomer Lake project is completed, Lakeview Road will extend straight across the lake and connect with Boomer Road. A new dam will have a spillway on the east end as shown. Estimated cost of the project is $2.24 million.
Drawing by Lynn Hazelbaker, Goss and Associates

The Stillwater power plant built on the edge of Boomer Lake in 1955 and 1956 to replace the obsolete plant on Fourth Street will get a rest of several years while the new lake dam is being built. It was located here because the lake provided inexpensive water cooling facilities. The plant will be upgraded while the lake is empty.
Courtesy of the NewsPress

Stillwater's first power plant, built in about 1905, was in the area north of East Sixth Street near the Stillwater Milling Company that will be commemorated with special landscaping. This was the site of the city's early water supply and of Morningside Park, a special recreation area and tourist camp for many years. Brick murals depicting early Stillwater history are among plans for the site.
Courtesy of the NewsPress, Pierce Collection

The Kameoka Walking Trail, dedicated November 1, 1987, could become a Stillwater tourist attraction. A horticultural area will feature a Japanese garden and later regions devoted to arid and tropical plants. Special trees, flowers, and shrubs will accent landscaping along the route. Located on East Twelfth Street north of Couch Park, the trail is named for Kameoka, Japan, which became Stillwater's sister city in June 1984.
Courtesy of the NewsPress

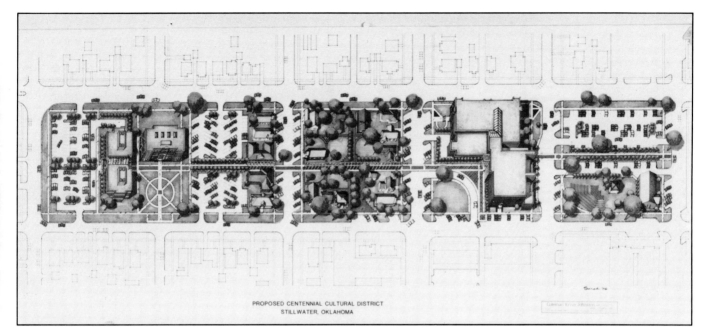

PROPOSED CENTENNIAL CULTURAL DISTRICT
STILLWATER, OKLAHOMA

One dream of great magnitude is a Centennial Cultural District between Duck and Duncan, and Seventh to Twelfth streets. A Civic Auditorium on the site of the middle school would be on the north end of the district and on the south end would be a museum utilizing old South High. Both schools and approximately fifteen pre-statehood homes along the axis would be preserved. Shops, offices, restaurants, and green areas would be spaced throughout the area. Winfrey Houston, attorney, and his wife, Barbara, originated the idea, and other citizens have joined in the effort to convert the dream to a reality. Drawing by Coleman Ervin Johnston, Architects and Engineers of Tulsa. Courtesy of Winfrey D. Houston

Stillwater citizens may soon bid a sad farewell to their public library at 206 West Sixth Street, shown here just after it was completed in 1938. The town has almost quadrupled in population since then and there are no adjacent lots for library expansion. The first library was opened in June 1922 by the Stillwater Women's Club in the former parsonage of the United Brethren Church. In 1926, the city purchased a home at Sixth and Husband which became the site of the second library. Courtesy of Bill Simank

241

A view from beneath this aircraft's wing shows an important dream for Stillwater's future. With the extension of the runways at left, Stillwater's Municipal Airport will be able to accommodate larger planes for direct flights to metropolitan areas. In the past, feeder lines to Oklahoma City and Tulsa have failed to create enough volume to survive. Flights by major airlines to Dallas, Kansas City, and perhaps other key terminals are among hopes for the future. Photo by Gary Lawson, the NewsPress

The future will bring a drastic change in this view, as the Stillwater Municipal Airport terminal building was being remodeled in 1988 inside and out. The airport officially began on December 7, 1929, when the city purchased 152 acres of land and a week later another 87 acres. It was at first called Searcy Airport to honor George Searcy, who was killed in a plane crash shortly after being named the first manager.

The airport remained largely a pasture until World War II, when OAMC became a military training center. At the request of the Navy, the Civil Aeronautics Administration in 1943 built the runways, and the airport acquired additional land to make the total 1,315 acres. OAMC leased the airport from 1949 until 1980, when the city resumed control.
Photo by the author

BIBLIOGRAPHY

Bassler, Clarence S. "Heritage Day Collections," 16 vols., Public Library Stillwater, Oklahoma. Scrapbooks.

Chapman, Berlin Basel. *The Founding of Stillwater, A Case Study in Oklahoma History*. Oklahoma City: Times Journal Publishing Co., 1948.

Comprehensive Plan 2010 Stillwater. Department of Community Development, Stillwater, Oklahoma, 1987. Xerox.

Couch, Eugene. "One Pioneer Family - William L. and Cynthia E. Couch," In author's possession. Typescript.

Cunningham, Robert E. *Stillwater—Where Oklahoma Began*. Stillwater: The Arts and Humanities Council of Stillwater, Oklahoma, Inc., 1969.

_____. *Stillwater Through the Years*. Stillwater: The Arts and Humanities Council of Stillwater, Oklahoma, Inc., 1974.

Debo, Angie. *The Rise and Fall of the Choctaw Republic*. Norman: University of Oklahoma Press, 1934.

"Early Stillwater History" Vertical File, Stillwater Public Library. Clippings, including memoirs of John H. Barnes.

Faulk, Odie B. *Oklahoma, Land of the Fair God*. Northridge, CA: Windsor Publications, Inc., 1986.

Foreman, Grant. *Indian Removal*. Norman: University of Oklahoma Press, 1932.

Hanes, Col. Bailey C. *Bill Doolin, Outlaw O. T.* Norman: University of Oklahoma Press, 1968.

Harlow, Victor. *Oklahoma*. Oklahoma City: Harlow Publishing Co., 1949.

Hudiburg, E. E. *Beside the Still-Water*. Oklahoma City: Metro Press, 1977.

Latrobe, Charles. *The Rambler in Oklahoma*. Oklahoma City: Harlow Publishing Co., 1955.

Lowry, Robert A. "Sketch of the Early History of Payne County." Stillwater *Gazette*, February 1, 1918.

McRill, Leslie A. "Old Ingalls: The Story of a Town That Will Not Die." *Oklahoma Historical Society Quarterly* 36 (Winter 1958-59): 429-445.

_____. "The Story of an Oklahoma Cowboy, Billy McGinty and His Wife." *Oklahoma Historical Society Quarterly* 34 (Winter 1956-57): 432-442.

Morris, John W., and Goins, Charles R. *Historical Atlas of Oklahoma, 2nd ed*. Norman: University of Oklahoma Press, 1976.

Morris, Lerona Rosemond. *Oklahoma, Yesterday, Today, and Tomorrow*. Guthrie: 1930.

Newsom, D. E. *Kicking Bird and the Birth of Oklahoma*. Perkins, Okla.: Evans Publications, Inc., 1983.

Portrait and Biographical Record of Oklahoma. Chicago: Chapman Publishing Co., 1910.

Rister, Carl Coke. *Land Hunger*. Norman: University of Oklahoma Press, 1942.

Rulon, Philip Reed. *Oklahoma State University - Since 1890*. Stillwater: Oklahoma State University Press, 1975.

Shirley, Glenn. *West of Hell's Fringe*. Norman: University of Oklahoma Press, 1978.

Sparks, Martin, Easterling/William Kessler Associates. *Oklahoma State University, Stillwater Campus Developments Concepts*. Tulsa, Oklahoma, July 1982.

Woodward, Grace Steele. *The Cherokees*. Norman: University of Oklahoma Press, 1963.

Wright, Muriel H. *The Story of Oklahoma*. Oklahoma City: Webb Publishing Co., 1929.

INDEX

ABOUT THE AUTHOR

A graduate of Oklahoma State University and North-western University, Evanston, Illinois, D. Earl Newsom began his career as a newspaper reporter and editor, then taught journalism at Texas A&M University and the University of Maryland. He was for a time administrative aide to United States Representative Lyle H. Boren. His four previous books include three dealing with early Oklahoma history, and the story of the great Drumright oil field. His years as undergraduate and graduate student at OSU after World War II provided an understanding of the university's colorful history, and his association with the *NewsPress* over the years brought him in touch with Stillwater's heritage and many of its pioneer families. He has been honored with citations for both academic and professional achievement.

As future Stillwater residents began the trek across the Cherokee Outlet, Robert A. Lowry described the scene: "The winding cattle trails to the territory being opened were moving, weaving ribbons of white-topped prairie schooners, flanked and followed by troops of horsemen." Four thousand schooners were in the caravan and hundreds of citizens stood watching the historic scene.
Courtesy of the Western History Collection, University of Oklahoma